ECSTASY
IN
AGONY

Dr. OM PRAKASH YADAVA

Contents

ACKNOWLEDGMENTS

Author is indebted to all his well-wishers who stood with him when he was fighting against the corrupt head and his followers in the ministry of defence.

PROLOGUE

It was the evening of first week of March. The cold winter had already said good bye and the hot summer was firming up its feet. Day time would be quite hot; though evening would be pleasant and the morning quite chill. The change of climatic conditions had brought their unwelcome effect and epidemic of swine flu and other diseases were gripping fast resulting into human sufferings and death, particularly in the poor class of people who were living in shabby conditions and lacked knowledge of preventive & protective measures. Though governments were claiming that adequate arrangements had been made to handle the situation but the truth was far from the ground reality and the government doctors were totally out of sight in rural health centres. Several NGOs (Non-Government Organisations) moving with their limited facilities & doctors were trying to render their help to hapless people in remote villages and other such locations, however, that was proving to be just peanuts. He had returned back home only a few minutes ago after having a very hectic & tiresome day. His wife had asked him to get washed & freshen up to take tea and relax. It had become his regular practice to get up very early in the morning, finish off his morning routine and be ready around eight O' clock. He would take his breakfast hurriedly, collect the lunch box quickly prepared & packed by his wife and rush to the clinic where he was practicing. He was doing his private practice as a service to the people and was charging his fee only from affluent & well to do people. In times of need he was extending his services to an NGO run by a social activist.

While sipping tea in the small verandah of the house and discussing with his wife how did he spend his day attending to patients, suddenly he heard the sound of ringing of his mobile kept on the table inside his bed room. He asked his wife to attend to the call. She went inside the house to respond to the call and came back with mobile in her hand and told the call was for him. He took mobile in his right hand and placed that over his right ear. He responded the call and was astonished to find a somewhat familiar voice on the other end but he was not able to place the same exactly.

"My dear friend, do you recognise me?" asked the voice at the other end.

"This voice sounds somewhat familiar to me but I don't remember whose voice is this."

"OK, try to identify."

There was a pause .... for a few seconds. Animesh tried his best but still failed to recall the identity of the voice.

"I am sorry. Though your voice is touching straight to my heart but I am not able to recollect and I don't think to have listened to it for past several years."

"You are right. You must not have heard me for the past several years but my voice had been very close to you as long as you had been in India and gradually the time & distance went on thinning the threads and I find to-day you having left behind the past."

"No, no; it is not so. Otherwise I would not have come back here leaving behind a fabulous life and career in the US."

"Could you still recognize the voice?"

"No; I am not able to lay down my hands upon. There were three-four persons very close to me and they all forgot me and their voice has also faded from my memory but if I see I can recognise everybody."

"OK. That is good. I request you to come to me, meet my mother. She is very sick and likes to see you."

"OK, I will come to you to-morrow morning. Please tell me your address and location details."

"No. To-morrow may become late, she wants you right now. My place is not far off; it is hardly ten kilometres away from your place. I will tell you the details and you can easily reach here in half an hour's time."

"Only someone very close to me can ask me like this, will you please tell me about yourself?"

"No. But you come and you will stand pleasantly surprised. I am telling you the exact details and you will reach to my house without any problem. I will be standing outside on the road and will receive you. Please tell me your car number. I request you to bring your wife also along with you."

Though not very happy, yet Animesh took down the requisite information and asked his wife to get ready to go to a place to meet some old friend.

It was an unusually wonderful journey on a typical Indian road. In the darkness manoeuvring ditches & dust, uneven unkempt pathway as much visible in the light of the car; it took him about thirty minutes to reach the place. In normal conditions it would have required hardly a travel of ten minutes. In the light of the vehicle he noticed a gentleman standing in front of a house who was possibly waiting for him. He stopped the car near the gentleman, opened the right side door of the car, got down himself first, taking a half round of the bonnet came to the person waiting for him and he was stunned to find the biggest unexpected surprise.......

The person waiting for him was none other than his closest friend Ratnesh.

"Oh my God! What a pleasant surprise. I am seeing you after more than twenty years. In fact, I had lost hopes of meeting you again. Ever since I have come back to India I have been enquiring about you but nobody could tell me anything about you!" Exclaimed Animesh.

Both happily hugged each other and Ratnesh hurriedly leaped forward & opened the left side front door of the car to welcome Anjali who came out of the car smilingly having watched how the two old friends had met with each other. They exchanged pleasantries and the annoyance whatever, Animesh and Anjali had felt while having received the unwelcome message of coming to meet someone not recognised on mobile phone, had totally melted away.

"Bhabhi ji, please accept the simple and informal reception of this poor brother and please come to my home."

"What do you say? A brother is never poor as long as he has abundance of love and affection for his sister."

"Oh, yes that I have but I don't have abundance of worldly assets."

"Don't mind, that I don't need."

Ratnesh took Animesh & Anjali inside his house which was small but appeared reasonably neat & clean. The inside of house was having two bed-rooms, living-room, dining and kitchen. One room was occupied by his ailing mother and the other was possibly being used by him as his bed room. Living room and dining hall were small having a few chairs and small tables. There was a big photograph of his late father hanging on the southern side wall of his living room, with a dry garland hung around it and an incense stick lit and smouldering kept below the same. The entire house though giving a very serene look was appearing to be a lonely place without any rumbling-tumbling of a child and without motion of a house wife. Ratnesh without observing any formality took them straight to his mother, who was half awake & half asleep. The sight was such that it totally trembled & shook Animesh from within and he got aghast to see the lady whom he had revered as the most beautiful & affectionate woman after the death of his mother.

"Oh! What a tyranny of time" thought he unto himself. And without expressing his feelings he put his head on the feet of the mother which was followed by Anjali as well. She opened her eyes and with a spark of blessings raised her right hand to greet & bestow her benedictions upon them and spontaneously he said, *"Mother, worry not. I have come and will see that you get back alright."*

"No my son. I had only one desire to see you before leaving the world and God has listened to me. I am happy and can go satisfied. I don't have much time left with me nor have any desire to continue."

"No, this is not fair. You are the only person in this country who is mother & father both for me. Ever since I have come back to India, I have tried my best to locate you but could not find any clue and to-day when I am close to you, you want to go away. No, no, Let God not happen this."

"Don't feel sorry or bad; everything is pre-ordained and God has programmed our journey of life, its destination, time & place of final departure. Feel happy that you have got me as I feel happy to see you."

"Ok, mother, whatever you say I accept. See this is Anjali, your daughter-in-law. She is also India born American, having her roots in India. She was very keen to meet you."

"My blessings to her, but where are my grand-children?"

"We have only one son; he is undergoing higher studies in US."

"Oh! this is my bad luck, I may not have any grand-child when I depart from this world."

"I am sorry but what about your grand-son and your daughter-in-law, Ratnesh's wife? I hope he must also be quite grown up."

Mother started sobbing, tears rolling down her cheeks. She was not able to speak anything. This further surprised Animesh. He looked towards Ratnesh, expecting some answer but he remained expressionless further deepening the

"My mother is counting her days and has been remembering you very much. Now I am satisfied that I could locate you and bring you to her."

"Do you think; I will allow her to go so soon? I will try my best to bring her back go normalcy."

"You may be able to prolong her days but nothing beyond."

"But why do you feel so?"

"You will know that as the time passes. Only I request you to give her, whatever time you

can give and let her pass her days happily and with least pains."

Animesh asked for entire treatment history, enquired about how had she reached the existing state of health and why Ratnesh was alone with mother?

Ratnesh told in brief everything about his mother but left the other question unanswered. Any way that was not the time to waste on some other issue and Animesh liked to concentrate on the treatment of the mother. In the meantime, Ratnesh requested them to take something as dinner with him and he went to the kitchen side while Animesh concentrated on the medical side of the mother. As he examined various medical reports and test results, he could evaluate that she was suffering from multiple organ malfunctioning & her life expectancy was very less and it was really a good luck that he could meet her but still he decided to take her under his medical supervision to do whatever he could. He along with Anjali sat by the side of the cot on which mother was lying and went on chit chatting many things of past particularly how had he been taken care of after the death of his own mother. He remained flying in the corridors of memories sinking & floating in many painful & pleasing moments. A time span of forty-five minutes to one hour had passed by when Ratnesh came and intervened.

"Dinner is ready, come and let us have it."

"First give whatever is to be given to mother."

"She is given some soup and one or two pieces of loaf."

"Is that ready?"

"Yes."

"Then bring it. To-day myself and Anjali will serve and feed her. Let both of us also avail this opportunity."

Ratnesh brought the soup and loaves in a tray and gave that to him. The couple happily took over the whole thing and as a professional paramedic staff served the mother and fed her. Somewhere in the deep corners of his emotions, Animesh was possibly trying to repay a bit of affection he had received when he needed that most and none of his blood relatives had come forward for him.

They had a simple dinner together after which Animesh and Anjali went back their home. Next day onwards they started a new life altogether; taking care of mother and also bringing food for her in the evening became a routine. On Sundays Anjali would come during day times also and try to organise everything in Ratnesh's house and also cook some nourishing preparations for the mother and do what all Animesh would have advised her for the treatment. After a fortnight's period mother started showing some improvements and she was able to talk properly. The changed medicines and the new course of treatment as advised by Animesh was showing its effect. This had brought some cheers to both the families but neither Ratnesh would tell why was he alone nor they would ask about that and the life continued as such.

One afternoon when Anjali was sitting with the mother and administering her some medicines suddenly she asked,

"Can you show me your son? I am very keen to see grand-child lest something happens and I go away."

"Ok. I will ask my son to come to India once his exams are over and stay with us for some days. During that period, I will show you my son - your grand-child. But excuse me why Bhai Sahib (Ratnesh) is alone; why his wife and children are not here?"

There was a pause for some times. Mother's eyes were filled with tears and with a very heavy voice she spoke,

"It is my destiny. I had everything, a happy life, my daughter-in-law and my grand-son but I have lost everything however I am happy that I could meet you and Animesh."

Anjali could realise that there had been something painful and she did not continue the talks further. She wiped clean her mouth with a wet cloth and took the empty glass of water and went to the kitchen. That night when Anjali went back her home with her husband, she told him about the discussion she had with the mother. He also felt a deep sense of anguish and expressed,

"Let us try to fill the gap as much as we can."

Animesh and Anjali were doing their best, devoting maximum time to the mother and her care. But some of the periodical tests being done on her were disturbing them and they were getting worried with the thought that improvement in the condition of the mother was possibly the last flickering flame of the lamp.

And lo! One late night there was a bolt from the blue. They had returned back home after having comforted the mother and having seen her slept peacefully and were busy chit-chatting with their son on Skype that there was a ring from Ratnesh in response to which he simply in a very feeble and trembling voice spoke,

"The light has gone off a few minutes back."

CHAPTER - I

JOURNEY ON THE ROAD OF PEOPLE

$\mathcal{T}$he gloomy thirteen days of performing all the funeral rites were over and normal life had to resume, moving away from the painful turn. Ratnesh had totally broken down and had even lost the will to exist, however, the comforting company of the friend couple was giving him strength to bear the shock. They had offered him to come to their house and live with them but he had respectfully declined; possibly he liked to be alone to merge himself with the memories of his past life. But his friends were taking enough care of him and giving succour.

Time is the best healer. It helps to forget everything good & bad and gives a new direction, a new dimension and a new goal to everyone; particularly whenever someone is passing through the bad phase in his life and that was happening with the three of them. Animesh and Anjali had returned back to their normal life and Ratnesh had joined a group of people who were devoting their time serving destitute and needy, poor people. Animesh was working very hard to alleviate the sufferings of the poor and needy people who were coming to him while his wife though not very happy with the life and attitude of people around her, was keeping herself satisfied to ensure the satisfaction of her husband. About six months passed by and everything looked as a part of routine normal life that one night he got a ring from someone,

"Neta ji (MP - Member of Parliament) has come to this town, he is staying at such a particular place; you come and visit him immediately."

"See, now it is late night and I don't know the place you mentioned. In case he is having any serious medical problem, please let me know."

"No, he is not having any medical problem but still you have to see him."

"I don't know, what for he wants me, but any way if he is so eager I will come to-morrow morning."

"No, he wants now."

"That is not possible. To-morrow morning."

Discussion discontinued there and he in his usual manner continued his normal chores and retired to bed. Next day morning he got up a little early, got himself ready and planned to visit Neta ji first and thereafter go to the clinic so that patients might not be put to inconvenience. With a lot of difficulties, he could locate the place of stay of Neta ji and he reached there. He found a big herd of people, some standing, some sitting, some chit chatting but all waiting for the Neta ji. He located his private secretary and apprised him of the message received by him last night and in turn was asked to wait. He expected that Neta ji possibly wanted him for courtesy meeting and may like to appreciate the services being rendered by him. He waited there for an hour, however, there was no inkling of Neta ji to meet him. He was getting vexed as he had never experienced such a situation in the United States where people were punctual to the dot and also he was feeling worried for the patients who would have come to his clinic. He waited for another an hour and only then there was a message for him,

"Neta ji is calling you in his chamber, go quickly and meet him."

He got up and willy-nilly walked towards the place he had been indicated by the messenger. He entered the room and saw a pot-bellied man of fifties, dark in colour but his lips were red and mouth appeared filled with paan, wearing Kurta and Pyjama sitting over a big cushioned plank. He saluted him who looked at him with askance and asked him to sit on the bench kept in a corner of the room. Two more persons entered the room and stood on the two sides of the Neta ji.

"Do you know that I am the leader of this area and certain formalities are to be observed by every professional of this area," asked Neta ji to him.

"Sorry, neither I know about you nor I know about any formality to be observed towards you." Came the instant reply.

Neta ji and his chamachas(flatterers) were stunned with the reply which they had never experienced in the past nor had they expected from any one and got vexed at him. There was a mute pause for a few moments and then one of his chamachas spoke,

"Then better you bundle up yourself and go away otherwise you won't be able to exist and survive here."

"No problem I am ready to go back to my country but you be ready to explain this to your prime minister because not only me but

all such people who have come to this country will inform him and pack up."

There was another shock to Neta ji as that was the most unexpected answer coming from someone sitting before him. He and his flatterers immediately softened their stance and in a mellowed voice, thus spoke,

"Are you not an Indian and how come you are here?"

"I am a born Indian but now I am a citizen of USA though I may be treated as OCI (overseas citizen of India). Why do you forget that during the visit to my present country your prime minister had given a clarion call to all Indians living there to contribute their best to their motherland and he had personally requested a group of specialised medicos like me to come and serve the needy people. Responding to his good intentions we left our lucrative assignments and came here and I hope you are a member of his party. In case I have to dance to your tunes then that is the end of it. I will inform about your dictates to your prime

minister and pack up but you have to reply to him."

That acted like a mountain of ice having suddenly fallen on a piece of desert land. Neta ji and his chamachas fell down from heaven to the earth and in a very very polite, meek and humble voice spoke,

"We are extremely sorry to have troubled you. We did not know of these things. Please forgive us and live happily here and whatever problems, please let us know and we will attend to them. Please don't tell this to the prime minister."

Animesh could notice the sea change in the behaviour of Neta ji and his flatterers but recollected the bad experiences of his childhood past which had encouraged him to leave the country and go away with a heavy heart. One thing became very clear to him that may be top leadership had changed but the people at the ground level were same what he had left behind over two decades ago and it was a good decision by him to remain as OCI without getting entangled in the emotional trap of mother land. Neta ji and his men repeatedly requested him for an apology and he came out of the room saying good bye to them.

Animesh hurriedly came to the clinic where he found people worried about him because he had never been even a single minute late in coming to his duty place and also someone informed them of his having gone to see the Neta ji. Most of the patients knew that Neta ji was a big fraud and his calling was definitely fraught with some ulterior motives. However, when they saw their doctor having come to them without any line of anxiety on his face they felt relaxed. They all wished him and exchanging pleasantries he went to his chamber to begin day's work. His being OCI and having come back on the invitation of the top person of the country had worked and Neta Ji never disturbed him again but life is life; it has many hues & colours. If one colour is neutral, it does not mean that its frequency & wave length will have no effect.

Animesh, though, did not believe in religious rituals but was not averse to observing certain norms which his mother had taught him in the childhood. He had a great liking for Lord Krishna whom he adored for His knowledge, wisdom, valour and practical virtues and used to visit Krishna temple along with his mother and also used to keep fast on His birthday - the Krishna Janmastami. Though they had become things of the bygone past yet their memories were pleasing and one fine evening he decided to go to the Krishna temple along with Anjali.

A famous Krishna temple was located at a distance of eight kilometres from his residence. He drove along with Anjali to that place. The journey was a blend of beauty & beast as the roads were horrible, full of pot holes and corroded traffic route, however, the scenes along the roads were fabulous and full of greenery. Though Sunday, still it took more than half an hour to traverse that distance of eight kilometres to reach the temple. He parked his car at an open place which was nearest to the premises. The temple was located at a hillock; they climbed more than hundred steps to reach the temple complex - a very arduous and tiring job to reach the abode of the deity. A large number of small-small shops were there selling POOJA MATERIAL and prasadam and were ready to take care of foot-wears of those who were purchasing items from them. They saw a small shop where an old woman was sitting and selling the items of worship. They purchased a plate of those items, removed their foot-wears and placed them in a corner as advised by her and marched towards the temple. There he saw separate queues of male and female devotees and accordingly they stood in the respective queue. The people ahead of him were marching slowly however movement in the female queue was a little faster. He gave all items of worship to Anjali and asked her to finish her pooja and wait for him at some prominent place and he would join her there. He took about half an hour to have DARSHAN of the lord and came out of sanctum to locate her who was waiting with prasadam for him.

"Did you have proper darshan of the deity?"

"Yes, there was absolutely no problem."

"But what about you?"

"You might have noticed the gents line was longer that took me more time and in the sanctum priest was not allowing to stand beyond a second. However, I had the darshan of the deity now let us go there and sit for some time under that tree."

Both of them went to the nearby Banyan tree and sat there on a bench made of cement & concrete. She offered him the prasadam which he took while paying obeisance to the Supreme Being. They remained there for ten fifteen minutes and then decided to leave the place to return back home. They went to the prasadam shop, collected their foot-wears and marched towards their car. They saw many beggars sitting on the sides of the temple pathway who were begging for alms. He felt too bad to find so many beggars and thought that,

"this country is having innumerable number of temples and other shrines and if every shrine is having beggars like this there would be innumerable number of people begging. I had seen such a situation when I was a child but surprisingly situation

continues unchanged. Then where is the change?"

Animesh was debating with himself and was totally lost in his thoughts that suddenly his sight fell on an old woman clad in rags sitting in a remote corner keeping her begging bowl in front of herself. That was a very pitiable, heart rending sight and his feet willy-nilly dragged him to her. He took his wallet out of his trouser's pocket, opened it and took out a ten-rupee currency note and put that in her begging bowl with an intention possibly to help her. Before he could take a turn to move away from there he found that a herd of beggars had flocked there. They also started asking him for alms. However, he was not very keen towards them. Suddenly he realised a beggar had snatched his wallet and they all began fighting amongst themselves to take away their booty of money from that. He noticed a police man standing at a little distance but he had turned away his face from the scene of that occurrence. After about five minutes when the wallet had become empty of money they threw it on the ground and all the beggars ran away. In that melee neither he could rescue himself nor recognise anybody. He decided to take help of the Police and approached the constable standing nearby.

"Please help me, some persons have snatched away all the money that I had in my wallet." Requested Animesh to the police person.

"What can I do, you should have taken care of." Answered the police man.

"You were seeing when the things were happening and I expected you would intervene and save me."

"No, No, I have not seen anything. I was busy in handling the crowd. What really happened?"

It was a great shock to Animesh that the person who was supposed to look after maintenance of law & order and who should have acted to save him from the clutches of unruly crowd of beggars was playing ignorant and giving him sermon to have himself taken care of. However, still in brief he told him what all had happened and requested him to help him but the police man, instead, advised him to go to local police station and lodge a first information report (FIR). He was not keen to go to police station but Anjali insisted to lodge FIR and they went there. It was located at a distance of two kilometres away from the temple. A head constable was sitting in the police station who was not at all in a mood to listen to them but when they told that he if did not heed to them, they will immediately call the local leader - the Member of Parliament (MP). Head constable was still reluctant to listen to him. He then told him that he was an OCI and if he did not listen to him that matter would ultimately go to PM and asked for his name. Only then the head constable moved and recorded the occurrence report a copy of which was given to him. The couple having tasted the effective system of police efficiency came back to their residence having lost the money, whatsoever they had. Though he remembered from his childhood experiences about the police system and how did they work but to satisfy his wife he had gone to police station and shown her their efficiency & efficacy.

Next day onwards he followed his normal routine forgetting the incidence of previous evening devoting himself to the service of needy people as usual. The experience gave them a food for thought to avoid visiting such places where every type of people freely come and go. A month elapsed but they did not hear anything from the local police. As advised by his friend Ratnesh, one Sunday forenoon he along-with him went to the police station to find out if there was any progress in the case. Fortunately, at that time police sub inspector in-charge was himself available and when they introduced themselves to him, he greeted them politely.

"You may be aware that some incidence had happened to me in the premises of Krishna temple and I had lodged an FIR. Could you please tell us if some progress is there in the case?" Enquired Animesh.

Police Inspector smiled and said,

"Sir, I have enquired the case. In fact, you should have taken the help of police constable posted at the temple premises itself who would have acted fast. This is a case involving beggars who are a sort of nomadic people and nobody knows wherefrom they come and where do they go away. But don't worry we will sort out the case." Elaborated the Inspector.

"I had immediately contacted the police person available on the spot. In fact, he had witnessed the happenings and turned away his face and subsequently advised me to lodge an FIR."

"Oh! I am sorry. I will look into it. Please go back, I will do my best."

He thanked the Inspector and returned back along with his friend. While on way back home Ratnesh clearly advised him not to believe what the Inspector told him and to forget the total incidence and the monetary loss, whatever he had. Several months had elapsed and he did not hear anything from the police and of course, he had forgotten that episode. The life was going on with usual morning to evening routine of examining the patients and doing his best to relieve them of their pains and medical problems. Patients had developed a great respect & regard for him which they used to express in many ways. He was happy to feel that he was serving his motherland and paying a bit of debt that he owed to the land of his birth; but Anjali was not very happy despite the fact that she was also born in the same land. She was missing the quality of life what she had been used to and the honesty in public life she had experienced in the other country. Their son, who was studying at Harvard School of Business was to complete his studies by the end of next year and was likely to get a good assignment in that country itself, was continuously pestering his parents to return back. However, they were requesting him to come and see the motherland of his parents.

One afternoon while he was busy in examining a patient with some serious problem, suddenly he observed a person with two others having barged in his cabin and before he could say something they occupied the chairs meant for the patients &

visitors. One gentleman who appeared to be leading the other two was wearing a white KHADI Kurta & Pyjama and the others were clad in normal pant and shirt. All the three had chappals as footwear. However, none of the three had courtesy to ask him to enter his cabin nor had courtesy to wish him. He finished the medical examination of the patient, advised him something and the patient went out. He washed his hands at the basin, wiped them with a white Turkish towel kept at the nearby hanger, came to his chair and occupied his seat. The gentleman appearing to be the leader, without any formality thus spoke,

"I want you to issue a medical certificate to (pointing towards one of the two persons) this person with me so that he can regularise his absence from his office."

"But I don't know you all and also the person has not taken any medical treatment from me and I also don't know whether he was really sick."

"This is none of your business. You simply do whatever I say."

"But who are you and what makes you ask me to do something so impertinently."

"I am the local leader of the ruling party and I order people to do whatever I like."
"Then there is no need of any medical certificate. You go to the officer of your friend and get the needful done. Any way I am not going to accede to whatever you want."

"It will not be good for you to refuse me."

"See I am neither a servant of your government nor do I expect any favour or benefit from you. I am serving the people on my own and let me do that."

"So you won't abide by what I say."

"You are free to feel so."

"Ok. Anyway I am going but that won't be good for you."

That evening he heard some noise outside his clinic - something unprecedented. He peeped out and saw that a small crowd of fifteen-twenty men carrying some placards in their hands were shouting slogans against him. He could not understand the provocation or purpose behind the slogan shouting. Suddenly he saw that leader like person who had come to him for issuance of a medical certificate was leading the crowd. He could then understand the reason of the crowd and liked to come out and talk to the people but the patient sitting with him advised him not to do so rather let them do what all they were doing. After ten-fifteen minutes the crowd disappeared giving a threat that if doctor did not behave properly they could teach him a lesson. Though incidence was insignificant yet it revealed that lawlessness was the order of the day and grass root level was not at all influenced or affected by the concern of the top leadership.

"What a national paradox?"

He thought unto himself of the preachings & doings of leaders and recalled the behaviour of teachers towards the students of poor, low caste communities while the books contained the preachings of Mahatma

Gandhi. What all he had experienced as a student of Junior college and the rough & demeaning behaviour of teachers towards those students had never gone out of his mind.

One evening he was sipping tea with his wife narrating her, his experiences with some patients who had come from a far off village, who lacked sense of hygiene and had developed some diseases for want of hygienic & healthy practices. There was a knock at his door and that was quite unusual. He kept his cup of tea at the small table lying in front of them, came to the door and opened it. A frail old man clad in rags was standing at the door who with his folded hands said,

"Sir, please help me. My daughter is very sick, she needs immediate help; for God sake, please save her."

"Where do you come from and what has happened to her?" He enquired.

"I am from a village that is not far off. She has got a wound which is deep and she is trembling with fever and pain."

"Why don't you bring her to my clinic tomorrow morning? See now darkness is falling and I don't know your village."
"I am a poor man and people told me that only you can help me. She is too much in pains. Please save her, help me. Whatever little I have I am ready to give you everything and throughout my life I will remain indebted to you."

In the meantime, Anjali also came there and looked at him from top to toe and enquired about his being there at such an odd hour. That old man touched her feet and started weeping. He requested her to help in name of God and save his daughter.

He could not understand what happened to Anjali that she got pity on him and asked Animesh to help him. He took his medical kit, some surgical tools, anaesthetic and antiseptic chemicals and a torch and got ready to move. They kept the lights of the house burning, locked the doors properly and came out. He opened the garage, took out his car and asked the old man to come in and sit by his side in the front seat to guide him the route. Anjali with all medical paraphernalia occupied the back seat. Slowly but cautiously they marched towards the village of the old man. There was no road, it was a rough dusty pathway with bumps & ditches. Really it was a nightmarish experience to drive on such a terrain, however, negotiating all odds they reached the house of the old man which was a small house made of mud covered with thatch. An old kerosene lantern was burning kept hanging on a bamboo pillar outside the house and an old woman was sitting outside on the bare ground. He stopped the car at a distance from the house. As they reached there she stood up with folded hands, full of tears in her eyes and started crying and praying the doctor couple to save her daughter. Anjali gave her assurance to do everything to save her daughter. The old lady took down the lantern from the hanger and asked them to follow her inside the house. However, that light was not enough and Anjali switched on the torch; in that light they moved inside. Hardly had they moved a few steps that on a small bamboo cot a girl was lying over a dirty blanket and she was mildly crying with pain. The doctor examined her from top to toe and observed that she was having high fever and there was a deep septic wound on her right leg just over the ankle.

"How old is that wound and how did she get that." Asked the doctor.

"About a week back while she was feeding my bullock she got that injury from the hoof and we applied paste of an herb which we normally use for such wounds." Replied the old man.

"That is a blunder you have done. It looks the hoof was having some dung sticking to it and with that it effected a deep cut injury. The wound has become septic and we can't say if it has developed tetanus. I have to do a small surgery immediately and after two days when she is able to walk bring her to my clinic for detailed investigation."

He asked the old woman to prepare some hot water and also asked Anjali to take out tools and chemicals for surgery. Hearing of surgery, the girl started showing her anxiety and reluctance and requested to avoid that and give some medicines instead.

"You don't worry, I will do something that you will not even know what has been done and there won't be pains. If this is not done your life will be in danger. Just bear for a few minutes. "Explained the doctor to the girl and the old couple.

Hot water was readied by the old woman and Anjali had made all preparations for the surgery. Animesh asked the girl to remain lying down on the cot itself in flat position and asked the old man & old woman to go out and wait outside. He prepared anaesthetic and carefully injected the same on the upper part of her leg muscle and waited for about ten minutes to watch its effect. He asked Anjali to focus the torch light on the damaged part of the girl's leg and carefully performed the surgery and removed all the damaged tissues. He noticed that the girl was feeling restive and occasionally screaming but Anjali took care of her while simultaneously also providing light for the operation. It took about half an hour for the procedure to be completed. Animesh administered necessary medications, stitched the operated part & bandaged properly. He then injected antitoxin serum and an antibiotic and called the old couple into the room. He gave them some medicines and asked them to follow medications as advised and see him in the clinic day after next day.

It had become quite late, though old man wanted to escort them back but they thankfully declined. It was really a tough job to drive back in the night but they had satisfaction of giving succour to some poor, needy person. The old man came in the afternoon of the scheduled day, however, he was alone. When his turn came, he met the doctor and apprised him that his daughter was not able to walk. Animesh asked him to wait and once he had finished to see all the patients present there, he would accompany the old man to his home. This continued for one more occasion after which the girl was able to move and after a fortnight she became alright.

One evening the old man, his wife and daughter came to his house. They had brought with them some eatables and other items. Animesh and Anjali were moved to see how much gratitude they were expressing to them.

"You have been like Lord Krishna to us. We will remain indebted to you throughout our life. This girl is the only light in our house; by saving her you have saved us. Please accept this what all we could do." Requested the old man to the doctor.

"No, no. Thank you. I have done my duty. If you want to give me something, you pray for my son. I want nothing. You please take back what all you have brought to me."

"We are poor people, we have nothing but whatever we have brought is my produce."

"Ok, I will honour you and take a little bit and that's all."

Animesh opened a POTALI (a small bundle tied in plain cloth) and took some puffed rice from that. He tied back the POTALI and returned that to the old couple and thanked them profusely saying that the same was a precious item for him as that was the result of hard work and sweat of the poor people. Though he had earlier too seen the goodness of the poor people of India but the old man's gesture reaffirmed to him that goodness was still the spirit of India.

"How old is your daughter?" Asked the doctor.

"Eighteen years."

"Is she educated?"

"Yes, she is matriculate."

"Why did you not allow her study further? I understand government has made girls education free up to graduation."

"Actually, she is our grand-daughter. When my son and daughter-in-law were alive, we had a happy life but in an epidemic they died a few years back for want of medical aid and since then we are helpless. In fact, she is

earning bread for us and I don't know what
will happen to her after our death."

"Oh My God! But worry not if you don't mind
I would like to help you. If you agree to my
proposal, your grand-daughter can work as
a receptionist in my clinic and I will pay her
adequately which will help you all. I will also
get her trained as a paramedical staff that
will enable her get a better job in future."

They thankfully accepted his good will
gesture and went back to their home.

Two years had passed by and the life was
going on in the same monotonous routine.
The only moments of happiness were when
their son would ring them and talk to them.
Sometimes they were also able to have him
on Skype depending on the availability of
network connectivity, though exchange of
information would be regularly through
WhatsApp. Anjali, though fully cooperating
and standing by the side of her husband was
not happy. She was a fabric designer and
had her own domain of busy activities. Here
she was not finding herself comfortable.
Though she was doing some job from the

house itself through internet but that was nowhere near to her satisfaction level and liked that either her son comes to India & settles there or she goes back, however, she was not able to express that to Animesh.

June was coming to an end and their son was completing his studies. He had been interviewed by a reputed company and was likely to get a good assignment. She insisted him to come to her at least for a fortnight after the exams were over, to which he readily agreed. It was the second week of July that their son Arvind was to land at the international airport. Mother and Father both had travelled in their own car a distance of about hundred kilometres to receive their son and were waiting for him. Arvind had been advised by his Indian friends to be extremely careful while dealing with different authorities at the airport as they could not be believed for their honesty and better if he carried a couple of bottles of liquor and offered them to enable easy clearance at the airport. He followed the advice meticulously, however, while having encounter with Indian immigration officers he was extremely careful and he observed that they were trying to divert his attention but when they got the liquor bottles they became friendly. Because of his careful handling, he noticed that one officer had tried to tear off a page of the passport of another co-passenger which he immediately pointed out and got that stopped. Subsequently he came to know that Indian immigration authorities play a lot of foul games particularly with Non-resident Indians. They tear off the main page of the passport and subsequently they and Indian police authorities blackmail such a victim and fleece away huge sum of money. Thank God! His caution had helped his co-passenger.

As he came out of the airport's gate, parents rushed to hug him and welcome him in their motherland - the country of their birth. They were *The moments of greatest ecstasy* for the parents and the son whom he was meeting after a gap of over two years. Mother kept kissing him for a few minutes and then took him to the parking lot, father carrying his luggage trolley and mother busy with the son. The luggage was loaded in the car dicky, they occupied the car, mother &

son sitting in the rear seat and father at the steering wheel.

"Let us go to a good restaurant and have some food as Arvind may be tired and hungry and I also feel like having something. Better we stay in some hotel tonight and tomorrow morning move to our place. Driving in the night is not advisable." Said Animesh to his family.

They agreed and proceeded to a good restaurant.

Next morning, they got ready early, had their breakfast and then moved ahead. The son had come for the first time to this country. He was very impressed with the Airport, its elegance and facilities but for the treatment of immigration authorities. The restaurant and hotel where they stayed were all equally impressive being much economic as compared to the country he had come from. As they moved out of the metro and proceeded towards countryside - the place of stay of parents, his impression went on declining. He observed the roads were in bad shape, traffic unruly and unlawful and people moving on the road unconcerned of the conveniences of others. On the way they stopped at a couple of places to take some tiffin and tea in road side DHABAS (country side food joints). The cleanliness and sense of hygiene were practically absent, although people were well behaved and preparations were tasty. The journey took more than three hours to reach their destination. It was very surprising to him as in his present country it would have hardly taken one hour to travel such a distance, whether it was country side or city.

Arvind was amazed to see the beauty and the great wealth of nature around the place where his parents were staying. He was very fond of seeing and meeting the common people of the country and accompanied his parents to meet such people. He found villages dirty and devoid of various basic amenities but simplicity of people impressed him. Mother made it a point to be with him for maximum possible time and his father also did accordingly. The period of the fortnight was too small and days & hours flew away and the last day arrived when parents had to bid him adieu at the same airport where they had been extremely happy to receive him two weeks back.

The usual routine of couple's life resumed and Animesh rededicated himself to the service of suffering humanity but there was something which was itching & twitching Anjali and mentally she could not be as before.

"Was something haunting her?"

XXXXXXX

CHAPTER - II

DESTINY DARES

$\mathcal{R}$atnesh rang on Saturday afternoon and expressed his desire to visit him next day. Animesh was extremely happy and asked him to come early so that they could take breakfast together and go for outing somewhere to relax and be away from the routine monotony. In the evening when he broke that news to Anjali, she was delighted as she had been feeling too much of solitude for so many days and was desperately in need of some refreshing change. She had heard of a beautiful lake and resort in a scenic location at about twenty-five kilometres away from their place and she made up her mind to go there, have lunch & early dinner and then come back by nine hours in the night. Her proposal was very pleasing to her husband and they started making preparations for the trip.

Ratnesh came at nine in the morning to their residence. Animesh and Anjali both greeted him heartily and told him of their plan. A light breakfast of boiled potatoes, eggs and sandwiches had been prepared which they took hurriedly and then packed up for going to the resort. It was fortunate that the road was not bad leading to that resort & lake possibly because of that being a tourist place. They reached their destination in less than an hour, took a room in the resort and booked for their lunch and requested for a simple early dinner. Anjali liked to have a change of clothes & wash while they were sitting and waiting in the lounge. They also had their face wash and along with Anjali took some light refreshment and cold drinks. She had brought with her mats, cards, biscuits and some other amusement items in a bag. They thought of going round the lake, enjoy the scenic beauty and locate a good spot and come back for lunch. In the afternoon they went to the selected spot. They sat comfortably, played games, chit chatted, enjoyed the company of each other and by sun set come back to the resort, took a light dinner and returned back home. The resort was located near a hillock in a very picturesque surrounding and was reasonably equipped with amenities. However, there was scant inhabitation around it. Lake was hardly hundred and fifty meters away from it. It was a very big lake spread in an area of several kilometres and was surrounded by dense forestation. As they reached near the water level of the lake they got immersed in different feelings forgetting the pin-pricks of day-to-day life.

"How the blue waters of the lake are reflecting the mystery of silence, mystery of that almighty who lives somewhere in the unknown depths of blue skies." Thought Anjali and became speechless.

"See the beauty of the whispering breeze, laden with melody floating over the waters of *this lake, are spreading their fragrance in limitless space of skies, what a wonder! Can we not find peace and solace in the truth of solicitude of these jungles?"* Was the instant thought which came to Animesh.

Ratnesh was also equally immersed deep in his own thoughts,

"How cool, serene, subtle and tranquil are these trees, creepers, grass and the lake waters. They are giving peace to anybody and everybody, whosoever comes to them in search of peace but why can't they spread their message beyond their realm of being so that world becomes peaceful?"

There existed a situation wherein each one had forgotten that he was not alone and was beholding the nature from his own eyes and his own thoughts trying to seek peace away from the hoodlums of life.

"Oh! Such a beautiful place, such soothing environs, such a mysterious lake; I had not imagined would be present in our neighbourhood. Why could we not come here earlier, at least we would have got

some respite from the commotion & bustle of our life and some peace, some comfort, some relaxation and some hours of freshness in the lap of nature." Spoke Anjali and that diverted the attention of both the friends. They spontaneously spoke,

"Yes, you are right. We have definitely missed what was so close to us."

While they were discussing of having missed such a heart rending lap of nature that suddenly she got reminded of a few lines of a poem that she had read while in the US.

"I once met a child who loved to skip stones,
Across the tranquil surface of a lake in northern Indiana.
One day, he went out on a boat
On that very lake, never to be seen again.
It's funny, those who appreciate life
Are usually the ones to go first.
I still sometimes wonder what happened to him,
But the world did not take notice that he was gone."

She then spoke,

"Be careful & cautious. No doubt, here everything is very good, everything which one can expect for peace is available but we are safe if we maintain a safe distance from the lake and observe safety norms to avoid wild & venomous creatures."

Ratnesh also supported her advice and said,

"Yes, you are right. Only recently some youth from a big city of Central India while on a picnic near a lake liked to have selfie while standing on the boat in the lake and met with a tragic end. The boat tilted on one side and they all fell in the deep waters and perished. No, no we will not go for any water sports nor even near the lake. We will only have the pleasing company of nature from a safe place."

They went on moving from place to place watching the twiners & creepers embracing their supporting trees; symbiotic plants flourishing on big trees. Orchids in bloom, green ferns near rocky locations and many different varieties of plants some in bloom and some bearing fruits. The environment was resonating with humming of bees, chirping of birds and the melody of the wind. As they moved further they came across a small clean place beneath a big shady tree which was cool, not far from lake waters and a small brook was flowing nearby. They decided to come there, sit and spend their time after the lunch.

It was a fabulous time being spent beneath the tree enjoying the melody of whispering winds, singing of birds, rippling of brook and rattling of dry leaves whenever some small creature passed over them. They were busy playing cards, chit chatting and munching savouries & snacks that suddenly Anjali asked Ratnesh,

"Bhai Sahib, when we were attending on your mother, one day she had mentioned that she had daughter-in-law and a grand-son. Will you please tell something as to what happened to them and also something about yourself that how did you reach this town since you are not originally from this town."

"There is a long and pathetic story but I will mention in brief without disturbing the happy mood that we are in." Was the reply by Ratnesh and he told his story,

"You know myself and Animesh both belong to same place and had practically similar life up to higher secondary education and thereafter our lives changed. My father was a businessman and my mother a social activist. I was the only son having lost my grand-parents in the early childhood and don't remember anything of them but my father used to tell me that they were very religious people and had always believed in honest business. Twenty-five per cent of their income they were regularly donating to religious activities and social welfare. My father also believed in those values and followed the practices of my grand-father. However, gradually the conditions changed in the independent India and honesty & fairness started vanishing from the business. Instead toeing to politicians became the order of the day but unfortunately my parents did not change themselves to such a practice and we have paid for that.

The local powerful politician belonging to the ruling party desired us to pay him the part which my father was donating to religious & social activities but my father was reluctant which won him the wrath of that politician. One day there was a raid on the store of my father by the officials of the narcotics department and they recovered some packets of drugs. The store was sealed and a criminal case was filed against my father. He was fined & jailed for a year. That was a very bad period for us and during that period we got support only from the parents of Animesh, who took care of us. My mother was very bold, she faced all the odds and restarted our business. We came to know that the whole case had been planted & manipulated by that politician as a revenge but my father had taken that as a loss of dignity to the honesty and a bane of new-democracy in the country. After his release from the jail he did not regain himself and one day suddenly disappeared and his whereabouts could not be traced. My mother without losing her spirit maintained our business properly. In the meantime, there were general elections and that politician licked the dust. While our situation was coming to normalcy, you know, Animesh had a shadow of bad luck and his mother died."

"Can you tell me how did she die?"

"It was extremely tragic. She was also a medico and both mother and father had very lucrative medical practice. Both were active members of the Rotary club & many other social organisations. There was an epidemic of bird flu and large number of Women & children were dying. On the request of a social organisation she participated in the preventive action and treatment program in the most highly affected areas and worked day & night. She neither bothered for her food nor for sleep. And see the cruelty of nature that while saving lives of others, she herself became a victim of infection and despite best efforts succumbed. That was the worst time for Animesh and his father. We were in higher secondary and that was the time when my mother came to the rescue of Animesh.

We passed higher secondary and our directions changed, while he continued in *science stream, I shifted to commerce stream. Our family relations continued unabated and most of the time Anjmesh used to be under the care of my mother. His father was keen to make him a medico and he had arranged his admission in the States with the help of his friends and after completing his graduation he went away."*

"Please tell me what happened to your family and your father?"

"We did our best but could not find any trace of my father and police also raised their hands. My mother stood firm and after my graduation she arranged my marriage with a girl from a family known to her. My wife was also from a business family and was very intelligent. She fully stood with my mother and our business was again re-established. I left my studies and joined with them and our family life was very happy & peaceful. A son was born to me and once he became a year old my mother started devoting her time to her grand-son and myself & my wife taking care of our business. Life went on merrily my son became twelve years old, he was a very lovely boy and very intelligent.

He was winning laurels in every field in the school but there was a bolt from the blue and our life changed. It was our destiny which laid its cruel hands on us."

"What really happened?"

"That is again a very painful story which happens only in this country. It was the day of HOLI festival; my wife had gone to her parents' house along-with son. My mother was sick and I had stayed at home with her. While HOLI was being celebrated with all enthusiasm, pomp and gaiety in the city, some miscreants sprayed colours on the people of another community who don't play HOLI and that caused communal riots and people started killing persons of other communities. My wife unknown of such a happening was returning back home and some hooligans of other community attacked my wife and son blowing them serious injuries. I came to know of that in the evening when they had been shifted to government hospital. I found them struggling for life; after two days my wife succumbed to injuries due to negligence of police and doctors. This ruined my life but

still I wanted to save my son and shifted him to another reputed hospital but the ill treatment given in the government hospital had worsened the case. He struggled there for ten days and died. I was finished and my mother went in comma. I had to carry on the funeral and also save my mother. Somehow my mother could be saved but our charm of life had gone. Though we came to know, who had killed my wife & son but politicians interfered and police did not do anything to punish them. My in-laws were very keen that I remarry and start life afresh but it was impossible for me to forget my wife. We stayed there for some months, sold out our property and shifted to this place. Some years passed by but we could not regain normalcy and my mother once fell on the cot she never stood again."

"Oh my God! So insensitive are the people here in this country, I had never even imagined. But what about your father, could you know something of him?"

"Once seven years passed by and he could not be traced police declared him dead and closed the file but still we had hope that he

must be alive somewhere. After the death of my wife and son, suddenly one day we saw a Sanyasi at our doors and that was my father. He had renounced the world and joined a monastery in deep Himalayas."

"Why have you come here now?" My mother asked him scornfully.

"I have come here to take both of you with me. I could see from my spiritual powers what all was happening here and now it is not good for you to live here." replied my father.

"You are an escapist having run away leaving us helpless, now why are you so much worried of us when I have lost everything in my life."

"That was my fate and it is your destiny."

"What rubbish are you talking?"

"Whatever has happened to us that was alotted and when I left away from here I was not knowing anything. Just my mind asked me something and my feet moved like that

but during all these years I have undergone great austerity & penance and have done yogic meditations which have enabled me to peep through the time. I could see what was happening and also what is to happen. I want you to avoid that but things will go of their own way."

"Then why have you come?" Asked my mother.

"That is again my destiny, I have to do that. Still I wish you both to come with me."

"No, I don't want to run away from the world, I have faced enough and whatever more comes I will face. My son has been with me and he will be with me." Insisted my mother.

"That is possibly the will of God! But ultimately my son will have to come to my place and take my charge, even if I am no more. Ok! May God bless you. Now I go."

In fact, I repeatedly requested him to stay with us for a couple of days but he declined and went away. I noticed a shadow of great disappointment & a pal of gloom on the face of my mother which I had never seen all those years and I had till then seen her as a bold, brave and fighter lady and even in the midst of toughest of the times she had stood steadfast. I could not understand the reason behind it but I found her a changed person after that.

"Can you tell me something about the father of Animesh."

"Why not. In fact, he was the only support to me and to our family. After Animesh left for States he had become all alone and was looking to see his son having become a successful surgeon. As Animesh's studies were coming to close he had become totally detached and was doing his job purely in a mechanical manner. One evening while he was at our house, he was quite morose and when my mother enquired about it, he simply said,

"My journey is over. How long I will be there, I can't say but I am satisfied that my son has become what I wanted. I can go with peace."

Next day we came to know that he did not get up. Some person from the hospital who had come to his residence to call him had found him dead."

"Oh my God! Such an end to two friendly people. Animesh had never told me all these things and in fact he never showed of having any such tragedy to his parents." Instantly spoke Anjali.

"See, past is past. Elders did their job with all their heart & soul. We have to carry forward the legacy with their values and our sincerity. Let us take the life the way it comes. Enjoy the sorrows the way we enjoy the gaieties." Commented Animesh and further added,

"My dear wife we have come here to live in present and not to waste time in going back to the past. I am following the goodness of our elders and that is all."

"Yes, you are right. Let us change the topic. Said Ratnesh better concentrate in the game, see I am winning."

"I know you were master in the game of cards and chess. We can't compete with you, we can only see how you play the tricks and enjoy."

"Yes. There was a time when I was very fond of these games but those days have become dreams. After many years I have touched the cards to-day. Thanks to Bahabhi ji but the old spirit I can't get back."

"No problem. Let us enjoy present with spirit of present but having inspiration from good things of past."

They had best of time up to the sun set and Anjali could know some of the facts which she did not know till then and that made her much clearer about her husband and his friend. They wound up themselves and came back to the resort. They freshened themselves and took the dinner and by eight hours in the evening left the resort on homeward journey. On way back while Animesh concentrated on driving carefully, some intermittent discussion continued between Anjali and Ratnesh.

"I don't know much of Hindu mythology but I have learnt that there was perfect understanding between Lord Rama & Lord Hanuman and Lord Krishna and Arjun, was that a friendship?" She asked Ratnesh.

"This is a very complex question and its understanding can reveal the crux of Hindu mythology. I can only say that in both the pairs one was human embodiment of supreme deity but he behaved as a normal human being and their friendship was based on unquestionable total trust & surrender by the other one and they together worked for the establishment of righteousness and for the good of humanity."

"I have also learnt about the love &relations between Lord Krishna & Radha while Krishna was a married man and probably Radha was also a married woman. Is it not an extra marital relationship and if so, then why such a relationship is celebrated and worshipped?"

"Bhabhi ji, this is something beyond my comprehension but what all I have gathered is that there was no mention of Radha in

early literature. It came very late and the person who is considered as the proponent of this, he is poet BOPDEV. What I understand is that Radha is soul and Krishna is supreme consciousness which is described as ATMAN and PARMATMAN. But I request you, not to ask me such questions which I can't reply you satisfactorily."

"Ok, ok. Do you believe in destiny?"

"I was a non-believer and always trusted in God and my own efforts but the train of events which have placed me in present position and also the events which have happened with the parents of my friend, I am forced to believe that there is some invisible force which controls us and our life and that is what is called as destiny."

"During our discussions near the lake you had mentioned that your father had told you to be at his place one day. Do you really believe that?"

"If I am destined for that I will have to go there one day."

Animesh was really finding interesting that his wife who had been brought up and educated in the States, where people feel all such things as silly was so much inquisitive about things which is prevalent only in India. And heart to heart he felt happy that probably that may help her to be little away from her inner disturbances; which though she never expressed but he had silently noticed on occasions.

Their town was approaching and they decided to drop Ratnesh at his residence and then come to their own residence. A delightful excursion, though, was over but Anjali had a new churning of her thoughts,

"Is really something like fate and destiny which controls one's life?"

XXXXXXX

CHAPTER - III

PAST PREVAILS

$\mathcal{N}$ilima- the grand-daughter of that old couple from the village was doing very well and in fact she was proving an asset to him. She was handling the patients very well, maintaining their records and case history, advising them properly for administering the medicines and scheduling their next visit to the doctor. She had developed confidence in working and the old couple was extremely happy the way she had transformed her own life and their life. Animesh was invariably taking her as assistant whenever, he was conducting any surgery and there also she was showing promising performance. Being highly impressed with her behaviour and performance, he advised her to pass higher secondary exam as a private candidate and also decided to depute her to Nurses Training Institute in the nearest metro, however, her grand-parents were reluctant to send her away. One Sunday he called them to his residence and during informal talks told them,

"See your grand-daughter is doing very well and she can have a promising future if she passes her higher secondary and also receives a formal certificate course from nurses training institute. Once she does that she can get a good job in a good & reputed hospital."

"But we are happy of her being in your clinic. Why you want her to go away?"

"She will not be very far off and that will be just for a period of six months and she can come & visit you on Sundays and holidays."

"But why you want her to do all that?"

"Suppose if someday I go away from here or go back to my present country, then you will not land in any problem."

"Ok. As you feel fit."

A famous government hospital in the city of the international airport was looking for a cardiac surgeon and one of the persons from the States who knew Animesh suggested the hospital authorities to contact him. A series of deliberations went on between them and ultimately he accepted the offer of the hospital and decided to join there expecting that change may help Anjali to find some better engagement opportunities for her. He also liked Nilima to accompany him and join there the training institute attached with that hospital. When Ratnesh came to know of that he got totally broken down and felt the same agony & pains what King Dashrath would have felt when Rama was leaving Ayodhya for exile. The patients who had been receiving treatment from him were also in tears and liked him to reconsider his decision of leaving the place but he politely told them,

"I am not going very far from you, every week end I will come here and continue treatment of all my old cases. And other cases who require surgery or advanced treatment can come to the government hospital and I will arrange all possible facilities."

He joined his new assignment leaving behind his family at the place he had been so far, however, Saturdays and Sundays he would be with his family and also attend to his old cases. That continued till he got a proper accommodation in the city.

The day arrived when he had to shift his family to the new place; all the people related to him in one way or the other had come to see him & Anjali off with tears in their eyes and prayers on the lips. He had retained the clinic and that was the solace to his patients and to Ratnesh. That day Anjali could realise where India differed from the rest of the world and despite all various plus & minus factors the Indians had an affectionate heart which pulsated for anyone who became close to them. While moving on the road to the metro, she noticed something very interesting that the lorries and trucks carrying heavy stores etc were having on their back a plate on which some logo, caption or slogan would be written. Those were very interesting to read. While some created amusement, some contained very deep thoughts. One such slogan became unforgettable to her,

"□□ □□□ □□□□□□□□□ □□□□□ □, □□□□ □□□□ □□□□ *(Ninety-nine out of hundred are dishonest, my India is great.)*"

That slogan jolted her terribly and stirred her mind vigorously,

"Why ninety-nine out of hundred are dishonest in India." was continuously hammering her.

Anjali had been born in India begotten of Indian parents but in the early childhood she had moved to States along with her parents and thereafter she had the life of that country but the household was adopting and following Indian rituals & they were Hindus to the core. While she had studied as per US curriculum, the family traditions and teaching of parents gave her lessons about India and religion & ethics as followed by people of their community in India. Her parents had taught her that honesty was the best policy and they had also told her the mythological stories depicting truth, honesty and sacrifice. While coming to India she had a longing to experience all those. Though at the place her husband had been till then, she had occasional experience of honesty and intensity of friendship but she had not been able to touch upon the facets what had been in her mind from the stories and legends as told to her by her parents. And lo! She noticed something which was extremely disturbing to her to read that ninety-nine per cent of Indians were dishonest. She did not ask her husband anything about that but she decided to understand the meaning of that slogan herself.

A reasonably good accommodation had already been arranged for their stay in the city where they made their residence. This place had good facilities of transport, entertainment and other amenities to which they were used to while living in US, however, the sense of public hygiene & cleanliness was totally missing on roads and other places. They were amazed to notice pieces of polythene and rubbish accumulated on sides of pavements and a poor state of garbage management. But they adjusted themselves to manage the things as moving in a car was not much affected by those things but certainly driving was not comfortable because of absence of proper Traffic sense even in mechanised vehicles. She noticed possibly the ninth wonder of the world that roads were used for anything depending on the sweet will of the users. Sometimes processions would be there, sometimes marriage Pandals will come up on the roads, sometimes certain jayanties (birth anniversaries) would be celebrated on them etc. without worrying for the inconvenience of bonafide users. Sometimes when they moved little away from posh locations they noticed a peaceful harmonious coexistence of humans & animals on the roads. Though she found almost all international brands of cars plying on the roads but their expected moving speed were beyond reality. Despite all those things people had no grudge or grumbling against the nuisances and were happy and managing every possible odd situation. That she felt as another wonder of real life in the subcontinent.

A time period of one month had elapsed and they had become a part of life of that metropolis. Though Animesh was still visiting his old clinic but because of heavy work load frequency of his visits were declining. Anjali had also joined some social organisations and a famous ladies club where she had become familiar with most of the ladies having powerful connections and luckily some of them were helping her to restart her profession of fabric designing. One aged but very powerful lady Mrs. Niranjan who was also founder member of that club had become reasonably close to her. Mr. Niranjan was a tycoon of infrastructure industry and was very close to the top leadership of the country.

"Are you really an Indian or an American?" Asked Mrs. Niranjan to her one day when they were chit-chatting in the club.

"I am an India born American. In fact, my parents belonged to India and I was born here itself but we shifted when I was a child and my parents permanently settled there."

"Have you permanently shifted to India?"

"May be no; In fact, my husband was very keen to serve people of his motherland as he always felt that he owed a debt to his motherland and somehow that should be repaid to whatever extent possible."

"Oh! So your husband is an Indian."

"No, he is also like me. He was born and brought up here and was here up to his graduation and after that he shifted for his medical studies but he was unfortunate to have lost his parents and therefore decided to continue in that country itself."

"How do you feel of being here in your motherland?"

"I am here by my choice and have a mixed feeling. Every person loves his motherland and I am not an exception but as a

professional I lack satisfaction not due to lack of opportunities but due to complexities of procedures and attitude of people involved in the business. I hope you could help me."

"Why not, definitely."

In the meantime, there was a call for Mrs. Niranjan reminding of her presence in some other program. She bade good bye to Anjali and left away. Anjali spent another half an hour in the club meeting some other ladies and then she also went away.

Anjali had got an assignment and she was keeping herself busy with that and obviously she had got some meaning for herself. Her work went on expanding fast but she was noticing something which was disturbing her. The persons giving her work were directly and indirectly asking her for favours, discounts and commissions and on many occasions they were deducting beforehand their share and only then making payments to her. Though she did not mind giving favours and discounts but other things were not to her liking, however, willy-nilly she accepted that as she considered better to remain busy than to sit idle or remain confined only as a house wife - a state which she had already experienced at her earlier place of stay. Her closeness to Mrs. Niranjan was also increasing with each passing day and they were sharing more and more of time with each other.

One evening Mrs. Niranjan on behalf of her husband invited Anjali and Animesh to her residence for dinner. It was prudence of luck that Mr. Niranjan was also present at his home on that day. A few formalities and soon they became quite informal and had a series of talks on various social, cultural and political issues of the two countries. Mr. Niranjan was very inquisitive to know about various aspects of life in the US.

"You have experienced the life of India and also that of US, can you tell us some discerning aspect between the two?"

"No doubt both are democratic countries and people are having similar values but one thing is very glaring that Americans do what

they say but same does not hold good with people of India."

"Oh my God! We never noticed this aspect but possibly you are right."

While discussions were becoming serious suddenly Anjali asked, *"What is the level of honesty among the people of India?"*

It was quite an unimaginable question and same stunned the Niranjan couple and they could not think for a while what to reply. There was a silence and nobody could realise that suddenly a bomb shell had been dropped. However, after a couple of minutes, Mrs.Niranjan handled the situation,

"See honesty is a product of society due to interaction amongst different cultural, religious, political and governing forces and also the value systems during an era and as such it is quite a complex phenomenon. Ancient India is famous for its honesty, values and social systems but things changed with the changing times. The originality of Indian systems got a total change after tenth century AD after which

the country was ruled by Turks, Afghans and Moguls for eight hundred years and thereafter for two hundred years by Britishers. These thousand years have witnessed many transformations and to-day things are quite changed. Though basically Indians are honest but their aspirations and expectations against the limitations have encouraged certain amount of dishonesty but still I can vouchsafe that Indians are God-fearing and reasonably honest but of course I do admit that government procedures and systems are such which encourage dishonesty and corruption."

"I appreciate that you have made a very frank, open and balanced explanation of the situation but one thing is continuously haunting me and that is while coming here from my previous place I had seen a slogan as per which ninety-nine per cent Indians are dishonest. Is it so?"

"No, not exactly. But definitely people at the helm of affairs in the government system are responsible for according such an identity to this country and possibly Indian railways and state governments are the biggest contributor to such an identity."

"Can something not be done?"

"Why not; if every citizen decides to be honest himself and does not succumb to any attempt of dishonesty or corrupt practice and also does not look forward for undue favours, things would automatically improve and existing systems would be forced to mend themselves."

"You are right, that is exactly what happens in US."

In the meantime, butler brought them the soup heralding that the dinner was ready. There was a showering change in the situation and both the couples who were entering into serious discussions got a change to tasty intake of fabulous soup. The dinner was marvellous and the affection shown by Mrs. Niranjan made them spell bound. Having enjoyed a delightful evening, Animesh and Anjali came back to their residence with some refreshing thoughts. However Anjali was still pondering over why is there an impression that majority of Indians are dishonest and what could be the factors behind such an impression?

Life was going on in a routine manner with Animesh having too much of work in the hospital which was giving him satisfaction of serving the people of his motherland and Anjali, though not very happy, yet was busy in doing her professional activities. The best part was the affection and intimate behaviour of Mrs. Niranjan which used to remove any sort of anxiety or disturbance, whenever she had. One day Mrs. Niranjan advised her to visit Lord Ganesha temple - a very famous temple of the city which was widely known for its benevolent & soothing effects of the deity for darshan (a glimpse) of which thousands & thousands of people were coming from far off places. Anjali, though was not keen to visit any temple or shrine due to what had happened to them in The Lord Krishna temple earlier but somehow she was feeling a mesmerising effect in the advice of Mrs. Niranjan and she, at length, decided to visit the deity on a Sunday or some other day when her husband was little free.

It was a Wednesday that somebody had advised her to be a very auspicious day for the darshan of Lord Ganesha and by chance Animesh had come back home little early and therefore she asked him to go to that temple to which reluctantly he agreed.

They changed their clothes and wore attire which normally Hindus wear when going to temples and proceeded to the shrine. It was a long journey of forty-five minutes that passing through crowded roads they reached the shrine. But there they found large serpentine queues extending on the road and no place for parking of the car. With considerable difficulties they could locate a place at a distance of half a kilometre away from the shrine where they got a pay & park space and they parked the car and marched to the temple. The enormity of queues disheartened them as it may take some hours to reach the sanctum. Some body advised them that there were a few entrances meant against payment and VIPs and they could use one of those to hurry up the darshan. Anjali repented that had she known of such a thing she could have used the influence of Mrs. Niranjan to get VIP pass and the only option left was to use payment doors but there also she found that some entrances were meant for bonafide ticket holders against payment of fifty to hundred rupees, however, they were also crowded. Somebody standing near a queue advised them to go to backside where a temple priest would be standing who would charge a sum of five hundred rupees per head and would take them immediately to the sanctum and would also arrange prasadam and all other formalities without any delay & trouble. Their life in the foreign land had taught them not to indulge in unethical practices but had also taught them the value of time and they decided to give preponderance to time and Anjali also remembered what all she was facing in her profession and they took the help of priest. That day they realised the power of money in their motherland and why corruption prevailed in that land. The abode of Lord supposed to be divine, most sacred, most pious, cleanest and most orderly was not valuing those tenets and obviously that message had percolated in the psyche of the people of the country. Anjali had got a reasonable meaning of that slogan that ninety-nine Indians out of hundred were dishonest and obviously what made them that. She had moved out of India along with their parents when she was a small child and had not known the country, its people, their philosophy of life, their value system, their way of life and their strength & weaknesses. She had known this land from a far off place through what all she had heard about it, read about it and seen through different people & programs. Her experience of living in the country was unfolding many aspects of life which were lying in darkness of her perception. A paradox she had found that people, though, basically good were facing identity crisis due to lack of national understanding and their struggle between means and ambitions and possibly that had generated in people a race against time and not only a race but a spirit of jumping over to win by hook or crook leaving behind the merit and strength of achievement.

Animesh, though having a good going in the hospital, was noticing certain distractions and interferences by generalists and administrators which was sometimes itching him. It was a Sunday forenoon that there was a ring at their door which Anjali rushed to open. She was pleasantly surprised to find Ratnesh standing at the door. She asked him to come inside the house and to be comfortable and called Animesh. They had exchange of pleasantries which followed with snacks & tea,

"I am very pleased to see you after a long time and want you to stay for some days with us." Said Animesh.

"I have deliberately planned to come here to-day so that I can stay with you at least for to-night. To-morrow several members of my organisation are reaching here and we are on a journey to Srinagar to help locals in situation of natural calamity. I have with me only to-day and that is for you." Replied Ratnesh.

"Ok, let us make best use of it."

Ratnesh got himself freshened up, changed his clothes and both the friends took chairs and sat in the balcony while Anjali got herself busy in preparing lunch which was going to be simple & light. They discussed many things of the news-papers, TV and gossip columns ranging from light matter to serious matter. Animesh was very keen to know many changes in the national scenario which had taken place after his having left the country.

"You have witnessed the changing times as a family man, as a business man, as a lonely man and also as a person selflessly serving the society; what are the things which have taken place after I left India?" Asked Animesh.

"Things have totally changed in the past three decades. During our childhood people had respect & concern for each other even if someone was new in the neighbourhood, now those things have vanished and everyone is self-centred. Though people say things have moved to nuclear families but I feel everyone has become a cocoon. And of course, let us not talk of the politics, that is not our field but one thing is very sure that we Indians are not meant for a democratic system of governance as for thousands of years we have been ruled by kings & queens and it will take several decades to understand the value of democracy particularly when everyone feels that he/she is a unit of a caste, a region or a religion."

Lunch was ready, Anjali called them to come to the dining room. All the three had simple yet wonderful lunch. In the evening Anjali liked to take Ratnesh to a famous garden to show him the beauty of that unique place but he was keen to be with them in the house itself. Ratnesh and Animesh had a lot of discussions of their childhood & adolescence particularly after Animesh had lost his mother.

"Your Mummy never allowed me to feel that I was without my mother. Everything that I liked to eat, she always prepared and sent to me. She knew when I would be gloomy and she invariably came to my rescue. Unfortunately, that human embodiment of affection is also gone." Animesh was lamenting.

"See! With her departure even the last iota of will to be in the world, I have lost. This social group has given me some meaning but sometimes I feel that they are also

working with some hidden agenda. May be I am wrong and wish to be wrong."

"Leave it. You do your job and dedicate everything to God! Almighty. I still remember once you had told me of what Lord Krishna had told Arjuna as mentioned in stanza twenty-seven of chapter nine of Srimad Bhagwat Geeta - the most sacred book of Hindus. I am also doing the same. And this thought keeps you unperturbed of what others worry for you."

"Oh! So still you remember that. Thanks for reminding me. In fact, the train of unfortunate happenings had totally alienated me from myself. I will keep myself busy with what I am doing till my inner conscience permits me. Rest I leave to God and my destiny."

Anjali again intervened to soften the flow of discussions,

"Bhai Sahib, I was told that you had been a good player of football and had represented your State and as a centre forward you were *invincible. Will you tell me some interesting episodes?"*

Ratnesh took a sigh, paused for a couple of minutes and then merrily spoke,

"Those are the things of the past - an unretrievable past but I will not dishearten you and tell you some of the Unforgettable events."

And he described several events and while describing them he went back into those days which were 'part of present' at those points of time. Animesh also supplemented and complemented his description of those events. Those moments brought cheers to all and they proceeded with a delightful mood to the dinner table.

Around ten thirty in the night they went to retire in the bed-room; Ratnesh in the guest room and Animesh and Anjali in their bed room. Might be two friends went into slumber but Anjali could not sleep for long. She was continuously thinking,

"How much we are attached with the past despite the fact that what happened can't be negated nor re-enacted but that is something which comforts everyone. Is it not a mystery of the God! Almighty?"

"But why this attachment with the past?"

XXXXXXX

CHAPTER – IV

MOTHER LAND HAUNTS

$\mathcal{N}$ext morning Ratnesh woke up very early and got himself ready to move away but Animesh insisted him to take breakfast and wherever he liked, he would drop him on his way to Hospital and willy-nilly he agreed. Animesh got himself ready, took breakfast little earlier than usual along with Ratnesh and he took him in his car. Anjali had still not come out of the thoughts which had haunted her last night and being alone in the house, she had allowed herself to be in complete grip of those haunting thoughts. She had the magical memories of her parents and the life in the States.

She did not remember of her life in India as she was hardly over three to four years of age when she had moved away. Her elder brother was ten years older than her and he had also accompanied them. As she grew up, by & by she got herself absorbed in the new set up of life but the house-hold and the religion remained unchanged. Parents would use their own language in the house and the religious rituals observed by them were different from that she would observe among people of America. Her parents would always talk of their village, their town, their people, their religion, their culture and of course their great country called India. Every member of the family would wear their normal Indian attire in the house, however, outside they would be dressed like other Americans. There was a Lord Krishna temple where family would go occasionally and there would be cultural programs on different occasions when the temple environ would look like mini India. They had a beautiful house in the outskirts of famous city Dallas/Fort Worth Metroplex popularly known as north Texas - one of the major business hubs of USA. Indians are spread in very large numbers in different areas of

Dallas, Texas. Her father was having a big garments outlet in a reputed Mall and was having a very good business. He had started off with the India-made exclusive garments and had expanded it to store a large variety of continental garments. How did he get the idea of coming to Dallas and start a business was not known to her. When she had become grown up her mother had told her that her grand-father was having a good business in India near Vadodara wherefrom they belonged to and he had encouraged her father to move over to US and start his own business with the support of some of his friends already well settled in US. Her father had once told her before the settlement of her marriage,

"When I came to US you were very small and your brother Anil was in the higher secondary class. His studies were badly affected as the curriculum in India was totally different but somehow we got him admitted in one step lower class. I started a small garment shop. My father used to send me consignments of assorted India made garments of all types, viz., ladies, gents and children. In the beginning there were no *takers. I studied the types of clothes these people liked and got them of that fashion and one known person arranged for publicity and gradually my business picked up. In a time-span of over ten years I became reasonably established. I got this shop in the mall and also started keeping garments imported from other countries as well. My Gujarati community continuously helped me and they also arranged for my green card. I was very keen that my father and mother come here and live with us but possibly that was not fated."*

She had a wonderful life in US, neat, clean and orderly but sometimes she felt herself and her family as to be grade two citizens of that country but the large number of Indian populace, whenever, gathered at ceremonial functions or other programs dispelled her that impression. She was showing great Interest in the designing of fabrics and technology involved with that and used to suggest her father about the changing facets of fashion which could attract market. She graduated with the normal subjects but thereafter shifted to fabric designing technology. Her brother did not like to go beyond graduations and he had become an associate of her father and taking care of their business. He had been married to a Gujarati girl whose parents hailed from Surat. They were also business people and she too had become a part of the family business.

Anjali after doing diploma in fabric designing technology had started her own professional endeavour and liked to expand her father's business, however, her father was interested to see her married and settled in her life. While he was in this pursuit of a suitable match for her someone suggested him of Animesh. He was then living alone and was serving a famous hospital as a resident doctor. In the beginning she was not interested in him but after a series of meetings both formally & informally she noticed something very different in him with lofty ideas and a sense of fraternal feeling for everyone, whosoever, came in his contact. It was this quality of his that attracted her towards him. They maintained occasional contacts with each other and after a year or so Anjali agreed to marry him. Marriage was celebrated in typical Gujarati style but Animesh was alone as he had lost both of his parents, however, an old Gujarati couple enacted that role for Animesh. After marriage Anjali moved with him to his place in Wisconsin and restarted her professional pursuit.

Animesh was much better and caring person than what Anjali had evaluated of him but one thing was hurting her that he would get extra ordinarily involved in serving his patients and may forget even if he had fixed any program with her, otherwise he would remain totally dedicated to her. She came to know of several cases which junior doctors could have handled but he personally devoted time for them. Though it was supposed to be a good tenet but Anjali felt annoyed whenever her prefixed programs were disturbed because of such instances. Despite all this he was liked by his father-in-law mainly because of his sincerity towards his professional as well as personal life and was coming up as a highly talented cardiologist in the hospital. After a couple of years Arvind was born which changed the life of couple and they started devoting more and more time to him. His first birth anniversary was celebrated by his grand-parents with great pomp & show inviting a large number of Gujarati as well as influential people of Texas. This was an opportunity which made Animesh a well-known Cardiac surgeon.

"Would you like to have your private medical practice; if you like so we can help you establish that?" asked his father-in-law to Animesh.

"No, I don't like that. I am well paid in the hospital service and I also get an opportunity to serve people. Basically I am interested to serve people."

"That you can do in your own practice also while earning much more than what you do in the hospital service. And remember now you have got a child and your expenses will go on increasing with every passing day for his bringing up and education etc,"

"That is true but Anjali is also having her professional pursuit and we will manage the things."

"Ultimate choice is yours but still you can reconsider the proposal and whenever you decide of that we will be there to help you." Father-in-law liked to know the views of his daughter also but she remained with her husband and the idea of private practice was deferred and after staying there for a couple of days they went back to their place.

The days, weeks, months and years passed by. Both the couple having a happy life with complete understanding for each other. Arvid was coming up in a very happy & healthy environ. He had passed the primary standards and was slated for next higher level. One evening Anjali got a ring from her brother that her father was sick and she was urgently required there. She rushed to her father along with Animesh and Arvind. Her father was very sick and hospitalised where he was found to be in terminal stage. Animesh used his contacts and they called the best doctor but sickness had gone beyond control and despite all possible efforts for a week, he bade good bye to the world.

Shock, a tremendous shock to the entire family. While she was terribly jilted & jolted, her brother Anil was in shambles. Cremation and funeral rites were conducted as per traditional Hindu system. After all the rites were over, her father's attorney came with his WILL which was read in presence of all family members and relatives as per which Anjali had been awarded equal share in his assets & business properties but Anjali & Animesh both declined to accept anything from that and they gave that to attorney in writing. By and by relatives went away and then Anjali, her husband and son also returned back to their place with a heavy heart having finished a significant and very formative chapter of their life.

Anjali did not remain the usual same rather a very vital change had come in her life after having lost her father and also having declined everything what her father had desired for her. She was fully concentrating on her professional pursuit and taking care of her son. She was practically detached from Animesh, who constantly noticed that change but he preferred to keep mum to let her have enough time to reconcile with changed circumstances. However, the change continued which alienated Animesh also and he devoted more & more time towards his profession and research work. Crisis is also opportunity, he thought unto himself and got totally immersed in his work which enabled him to develop a new technique of cardiac surgery and the papers published by him were highly appreciated. In that situation a time span of five years passed by and only their son made them realise that; when he expressed his desire to go for higher studies away from them as a boarding student. That awakened them to look at their changed lives, either to be poles apart or come together to relive a happy life. Luckily good senses prevailed and they decided to reopen their old chapters. Money was in abundance with them and name and fame was also in plenty and without worrying for those things they started again living caring for each other.

Animesh had a great concern for senior citizens and whenever such cases were coming to him he was taking additional care, but something was disturbing him. In his mother land he had been taught and had also seen children taking care of their parents and grand-parents while living in a joint family. When someone fell ill whole family would take care of him or her but in his present country that system was not visible. Most of the senior citizens who came under his treatment were residing in old age homes and he was astonished to find them uncared for and virtually abandoned by family members, at a time when actually they needed them most. In some instances he felt pained to notice that family members were nowhere in sight when the patient was leaving the world for his or her eternal abode. But the care taken by him, other doctors of the hospital and staff members and also by state authorities were par excellent. In several cases children came to enquire only when the cremation had already been arranged by the state. What an irony & paradox in the most developed nation on the globe?

Arvind had gone away to stay at college boarding in another place and due to his absence Anjali & Animesh had changed themselves giving maximum available time to each other without affecting their professional pursuit. Several years passed by getting them in their own life with their son going up & up each year scaling newer heights. In the initial years his visit to parents' was quite frequent but gradually that became twice a year only during long vacations or when owing to extremely inclement weather schools & colleges would be closed indefinitely. He had shown extremely brilliant performance adding glory to himself and of course proud moments to his parents.

His father was quite desirous that he also becomes a surgeon and takes ahead the field where he had earned laurels but he was not showing any interest in such a field and disliked tearing off dead or alive bodies, however, he was not expressing that to his father but had given indications of his likings to his mother. He had appeared in the final year exams of the college and had come to see his parents for a week that he expressed his liking for going to business management. Willy-nilly Animesh endorsed his desire but added that if he was really going to pursue a career in that field he must try hard and get an admission in Harvard School of Business.

Animesh had always believed in hard work to hit the bull's eye and was sanguine that his son won't disappoint him.

"Did that happen?"

"The bell of time rang and replied, yes."

One evening Anjali asked Animesh to go out in the nearby park and therefrom to the famous restaurant to take dinner. The park was one of the most beautiful places and for a long time they had not been there or anywhere else outside the home together. It was very refreshing to watch the tulips in bloom, some yellow, some violet, some orange, some red and astonishing some whitish, all planted in separate rows. Hundreds of meters long rows extending from one end to the other end of the park. They were walking enjoying the splendour of the flowers and majesty of the colourful plants that suddenly Anjali asked,

"Do you still love me?"

"Why? Why, have you any doubt."Replied Animesh.

"See, over last five years we have gone on our own way just having a compromise of being under the same roof. In fact, in such a situation any young American couple would have taken divorce long back."

"That is their way of life. I am not a born American, my way of life is still Indian and that too a Hindu way of life. Marriage is life-long partnership between the husband & wife equally sharing pleasures & pains. I knew you were in shock which had diverted your attention to seek solace in your son and your professional pursuit. Let me also share frankly that whatever breakthrough I could achieve in my field was also possible only because of your diversion away from me and in that situation instead of getting frustrated I devoted my entire energy in my research work."

"Oh! So kind of you. Let us be clear and restart with a clean slate."
"Ok."

"Sometimes memories of my childhood haunt me and I feel restless. Can we find an occasion to have a visit to India particularly to the place where my father had lived when I was a child?"

"I have nobody in that country and a few close friends whom I had during student life, have also become unknown. Neither I know their whereabouts nor did they try to find me out. Your position is not different from me; then why do you feel like going there?"

"Even then some faint & vanishing memories are there which call me. Pictures of my father and how he was nurturing me comes to my mind. Why not we find some pretext and go there for a few days."

"If some opportunity comes of its own we will definitely go there. But I will not create on my own."

They happily enjoyed the moments of togetherness in the park, went to the nearby popular restaurant serving Indian food & cuisines and having got themselves refreshed came back home with an un-forethought idea of visiting their motherland sometimes in future.

Anjali was surprised from her own proposal and was feeling askance to get unmindfully an idea of visiting her motherland and the place where her parents had lived once upon a time. She was having extremely faint idea of her place where she lived as a small child and had never thought of any such rendezvous but then she thought, "*God never does something without a purpose*," and may be that is harbinger of something in the womb of time. Though she was not encouraged by Animesh to create an opportunity to go to India but she thought,

"*Let me see, what does God like?*"

<u>xxxxxxx</u>

CHAPTER - V

ASTONISHING EXPERIENCES

$\mathcal{T}$he prime minister of India who had come with a thumping majority after several decades of shaky governments, was visiting US and meeting various strata of Indian community settled & well established in that country. He was giving a clarion call to all people of Indian origin to contribute their humble might to serve their country of origin in whatever way they could. There was so much of magnetism in his request that every person of such communities was going to do his best. A group of doctors serving in different places and in different capacities decided to leave their assignments in the US and go to India to serve the needy people there. This group approached the visiting dignitary and put their proposal to him which was readily welcomed.

Animesh, though not keen to join that group of doctors, remembered the desire of Anjali to visit her homeland and joined the group of all such doctors & surgeons who came to India and went to different places of their liking. He preferred to serve poor people and destitute, who were far from availability of modern facilities and expert doctors. So he came to a small town and did his best but he was astonished to notice that India was no more the old country where people had care & concern for helpless people, rather the politicians were ruling the rut and without their blessings it was difficult to do even selfless good work. And that observation gave him a shock, a jolt but any way as long there was no interference in his work, he did not care for that.

However, he got an opportunity in a big hospital in a metropolis and he opted to join there with the thought that he would be able to perform major life saving surgeries and also he had in his mind to help poor people suffering from major cardiac problems - something spreading like an epidemic in India. He started in the new environ on a very happy note and his wife also got a diversion. She had started doing some work from her residence and whenever she was going to ladies' club, she was able to have an exchange of thoughts with different ladies and particularly her relations with Mrs. Niranjan were very rewarding.

A young patient from an affluent family had got admitted in that hospital having abnormal enlargement of heart. Most of the reputed cardiac surgeons had refused to touch that case as the chances of rectification through surgery were minimal and it was very likely that patient may collapse on the operation table itself. The superintendent of the hospital was worried about the patient as there was pressure on him regarding that case being cured. At length he requested Animesh,

"Doctor, there is a very difficult case, I know, but can you try and save him?"

"Get me all the relevant papers and let me thoroughly examine the case."

Animesh was given all the relevant details and the opinion of some other reputed cardiac surgeons. He found that to be a very difficult case but still had a ray of hope to handle that. He liked himself to get all the previous investigations redone including CT angiography. He himself examined the mental state of the patient to see whether he had the fighting spirit to undergo the rigours of surgery and survive. Having satisfied himself with the new series of tests and their observations he met the superintendent and said,

"No doubt, this a very serious case fraught with failure but I would like to take a chance and hopefully it may turn out to be success."

"Very good. Do you need some help?"

"Yes. I want associates of my choice whom I know very well and then faith of the family members of the patient in God and me."

"First part will be arranged and second part will be conveyed."

"Thanks."

Having done all the calculations and precautions the surgery was conducted on a normal working day. It was a very lengthy and strenuous operation where surgeon had to be extremely cautious & careful and meticulous in every procedure involved therein. It took more than four hours to complete the surgery, at the end of which the entire team involved in the surgery took a sigh of relief, however, patient was to be meticulously observed for next seventy hours in the cardiac care unit. Thank God! the observation period passed off without further complications and patient showed signs of recovery and lo! after a week's period he was reasonably recovered. This was an amazing success which made Animesh overnight one of the most famous & outstanding cardiac surgeons. Thereafter the journey of his success story continued unabated. Rich and poor, everyone whosoever, suffered from cardiac problem was desirous to avail his services and he equally took care of every patient. This situation had given him a sense of satisfaction and he felt that his decision of coming to India was possibly right.

But India is India - a land of its own peculiarities and unpredictable turns. A poor man met him one Sunday evening at his residence and requested him for his help.

"Sir, I am a poor man and have only son, thirty-five years old. He has been identified as a cardiac patient and is in serious need of surgical intervention. I have been to several hospitals, but people are demanding a huge sum of money for the surgery which I can't afford. I have knocked at the doors of several NGOs but not too much help. Except that one NGO who has come forward to help me and that is also just a part of expenses. I have heard enough of you and I have come to you as the last citadel of my hopes & prayers. Will you please help me?"

"You come to me with your son to-morrow in the hospital. Let me examine him and see what can be done."

Next day that father-son duo came to him as a registered case of that hospital. He examined all his previous examination reports and found that to be a case of deformation of ventricular valve. As a result, deoxygenated blood was getting mixed with oxygenated blood of auricles. This was also a very serious case and an open heart surgery was called for repairing the deformed valve. This involved a costly and lengthy surgical procedure and the help, which he was likely to get from the NGO was not at all enough. Something happened and Animesh developed an interest to help that father by treating his son. He contacted a Christian social organisation who had become quite familiar to him and had helped a case earlier. It was prudence of luck that they agreed to help that case too. Detailed reinvestigation of the case was done and having satisfied all the pre-requisites the surgical operation of the case was fixed on a Thursday. He himself was going to lead the team of doctors along with his trusted aids. The procedure had been started, sternum cut and rib cage opened for further delicate and sensitive procedures. At that point of time he got an urgent call from the hospital superintendent to see him. He explained the whole situation and liked to come to him after the major surgery was over but he was forcefully asked to come there just for a couple of minutes. He was extremely annoyed but still leaving the case to his aid he took off the OT (operation theatre) attire and went to superintendent. He found there some politician sitting with the superintendent.

"See, he is Mr.Jutawala - the most influential public figure of the area and he has a serious cardiac problem, just attend on to him." Said the superintendent.

"I am having a very serious case whose rib cage is already open, if this gentleman can come in the afternoon or to-morrow morning, I can examine him with full devotion." Replied Animesh.

"No, no, he is not a person who can be asked to wait. Your case I know, that can wait for a few minutes. Your subordinates will handle. It is matter of a couple of minutes, just you examine him and go back."

He unwillingly obeyed the superintendent and started examining the case of the politician. It was a simple case which other cardiologists of the hospital could have dealt with easily but gentle man was unnecessarily wasting his time and took thirty minutes to complete the examination and after which Animesh could return back to the operation theatre. That openness of heart had worsened the case. He did his best, carried on the procedures on the heart and repaired the damaged valve but he was apprehensive of secondary infections and invisible damages due to undesirable exposure of the heart. And that really happened and after two days of surgery, the young patient collapsed who otherwise was a fit case of success & survival. He was made a target of media and was made responsible for the failure. All good work done by him so far went into dust and the high handed behaviour of the hospital superintendent was not highlighted. Niranjan family came to know of that and were disturbed. They called a press conference and highlighted the role played by Animesh till then and unscrupulous orders of hospital superintendent to leave the patient on the operation table and obey his orders but they also did not mention any thing about the politician and the role played by him. Superintendent took it as his insult and he called Animesh to his cabin,

"Why did you arrange a press conference against me?"

"That I did not do, better you ask Mr. Niranajn."

"He is your friend and must have acted on your instance."

"No doubt he is my friend but what did he do better ask him."

"I can't accept that he did that on his own, you must have instigated him."

"Better please don't repeat the same question but it is beyond doubt that you are really the person who is responsible for death of that patient."

"I damn care such patients. Such people die every day in hundreds and I can't care. It is *because of you that the case became a media favourite."*

"Yes, for me every patient is important. I regret that a poor man who could have been saved died because of your stubborn attitude."

"See, I have to take care of those who matter for me and my hospital. I cannot afford wrath of a powerful person who can do a lot. Insignificant persons like that patient, whether they survive or die is not important for me nor for this hospital. If you feel so bad you are most welcome to go."

It was a tremendous shock to Animesh. He had left behind a prosperous life & career and had come to his mother land with dedication and devotion to serve people who needed his expertise but he was disappointed to receive such a frugal response from a person who was supposed to be the pillar of the hospital. He felt dejected & frustrated also of having left his clinic in the small town where he was his own boss, though he had seen the nuisance of politicians there as well. He consulted the

Niranjan family and tendered his resignation from the service of that hospital. Only then the superintendent did realise his mistake but that was too late.

He subsequently joined another reputed hospital run by a trust. The facilities were much better there and he was most welcome as his reputation was going to attract more and more number of affluent patients to that hospital. His emoluments and perks were also much higher as compared to his previous assignment. He got a very nice treatment in the new hospital and got himself firmly set with his job. He was handling most difficult cases with cent per cent success which attracted many patients from the middle-east countries adding laurels to the hospital. But one thing haunted him, that he was not getting any poor person either for treatment or for rendering them any help. That used to pain him immensely, but he had satisfied himself with the professional satisfaction that he was getting.

His son Arvind had completed his Masters in Business with flying colours and had joined a reputed company as an important executive. He was continuously pestering his parents to finish their sojourn in India and come back. He was feeling that they have done enough and that was all. A large number of articles used to come in US media showing horrific state of women security, miserable plight of children and murders of senior citizens in India and he was quite worried about the well-being of his parents. A news became highlight of the international media when two young girls were raped, murdered and their dead bodies hanged on a tree in some town of Uttar Pradesh, a northern state of India and even subsequent to that nothing meaningful had been done by the government. In fact, US media had been relentlessly bringing out the horrors of atrocities on women, children and senior citizens in the capital city of the country and elsewhere. He also found that people of north east had become victims and being murdered in Delhi and tourists coming to India were also not very safe and all such news items were worrying him. He knew that his parents were no longer Indian citizens and being straight forward in their approach & outlook, they could not be safe in that country. He, at length, gave an ultimatum to his parents that if they did not decide to come back or indicate a firm time frame of their return he will himself come and take them back. In the meantime, they came to know that an affluent Gujarati family was keenly interested in fixing marriage of their daughter with Arvind and they were also waiting to see them back in US.

Animesh was reasonably satisfied with the sense that his expertise was getting a meaning and several cases which could have gone abroad had been treated well in the country itself. Over a year had passed and he had a feeling that the present hospital was a better place that suddenly an episode jolted him. There happened an instance that two patients in a general ward expired while they were undergoing infusion of dextrose-saline after a normal surgery. That case had not been given much ado and was attributed to drug reaction causing fatality but after a few days about a dozen casualties occurred under the similar circumstances. This episode attracted media attention which led to formal enquiry. It was found that a substandard contaminated store had been used which had been manufactured and supplied by a firm already blacklisted by the government. The detailed examination revealed a nexus between procurement division of the hospital and the supplier. That was another shock which totally uprooted the very foundation stone of his faith in the Indian medical ethos and how the lives of poor men were evaluated and of course identified. He could know that all those belonging to affluent & rich families were purchasing all medicines and other paraphernalia required for their treatment from outside drug stores as prescribed by the doctors and obviously there was no problem with their quality. It were only the poor people who were becoming victims of greed & corrupt practices of unscrupulous elements of the hospital. But he had a feeling that top brass of the system was not involved in those acts. A few months more passed by and the formal findings of the enquiry had come out which revealed some unimaginable facts showing involvement of some of the most responsible persons of the hospital.

The divine feeling of service with which he had come to motherland was fading away due to his continuous observation of lust and greed in the people whom he revered and believed to be honest & responsive and finding them involved in inhuman activities that too just for the gain of some unethical benefits. He remembered his childhood and the school where he was studying in eighth standard. He was the most meritorious student scoring cent per cent in all the subjects and all the tests of the class, however, in the final examination another student who was never in forefront came first in the class and the same thing repeated in the next standard also but in the matriculation examination which was conducted by an authorised independent agency he topped the merit list whereas the other boy was nowhere in sight. He liked to know why such a thing had happened during previous two years and was stunned to know that the other boy was in direct relation with the principal of the school and all teachers were forced to favour him. A similar situation he had faced in subsequent years in the practical examinations of different science subjects. Though he was never unnerved with such instances but he had lost the reverence to the teachers about whom he had been taught by his parents in the childhood that, *A teacher is like God.* And that thought vis-a-vis his own observations in the school and college hammered his mind and when he came to know that teachers in western countries never indulged in such practices and merit & performance of a student was always encouraged. Somewhere that thought lying deep in the psyche of Animesh prompted him to go abroad for higher studies and subsequently circumstances catalysed him to become a citizen of that country. However, he was baffled that the land known as the great country of sages had got so much transformed and the citadels of great human concern like health and education had also become adulterated with negative values. Alas ! why that happened,

"Was there something wrong with the wind, soil and water of this country?"

<u>**xxxxxxx**</u>

CHAPTER - VI

DISMAY

Animesh was riddled the way his belief that things would have changed in his motherland had been belied. Still he had some hope that the top leadership, the way it was interested to take country to greater heights would act to improve upon the situation, but unfortunately he had forgotten that system available in the country was full of antihistamines which broke vertical communication to the nerve centre of the country. Arvind though settled properly was constantly soliciting his parents to return back and the parents of the girl who were interested in matrimonial alliance were too anxious to see them back at the earliest. Animesh was in a dilemma and liked to have little more time to firm up his mind. One afternoon when he had completed his surgeries allotted for the day and was just relaxing in his cabin he received an envelope through postal dak. He found that to be an inland envelope carrying his address without details of the sender. However, the hand writing of the address seemed familiar. He opened the envelope which contained a short handwritten message reading,

Dear Anu,

My association with the active worldly life looks to be short lived. You know that I have lost everything in my life, my father, my wife & son and my mother. Even the business which was the source of bread has also got damaged. My father-in-law was very keen to get me back in life and restart my business but the place where I had lived happily with my family was always reminding me of them and I liked to be away from that trauma and for that reason I deliberately left that place also. In order to make my life useful to society I joined this serving organisation but I am totally dismayed.

We had started on a very positive note with sense of dedication but as the Organisation grew more and more people joined it and gradually inter personal differences arose due to clash of interest. A situation has come that except those who have been the first group of people the others, who are now in majority, are interested more in political ventures and availing different grants from the governments.

I have gradually lost the last straw of hope by catching at which I had thought of making rest of my life for others. Probably that is my destiny and it looks that I may have to renounce the world and adopt the path what my father had adopted. In the coming few days I will make myself clear of what I have in my mind, however, before bidding adieu I will like to meet you.

Please convey my best wishes and thanks to Bhabhi ji.

Regards
Ratnesh.

The letter was very clear that Ratnesh had made up his mind to act fast. He knew him as a man of determination and once he had decided something it won't be possible to change him and it was only that he need be encouraged to pursue his path. In fact, Animesh was also in dilemma whether to continue in the environment where his faith and belief were being shattered and honesty was not the national ethics and repeat the same story which he had done at the end of his graduation; but still he liked to have one more chance and may be the last chance. However, he never showed in the hospital that his mind was disturbed with certain happenings and continued the way he had been doing his professional work and another month's time passes by.

A minister of the state government had been shifted from the government hospital to his hospital for specialised treatment of a pulmonary disease and the experts were attending on him. He was having pain in his chest and had been briefed that pain would be there but every now and then he would be asking for Animesh to come to him and check-up and ensure that he did not meet with any cardiac arrest. He had already been thoroughly checked and there was nothing to worry on cardiac front but still he was troubling Animesh often and on. Once one of his flatters came to call him,

"You are immediately required to examine the Sir. Leave all other work and come with me." He asked Animesh.

"I know his problems, the pain in his chest is not due to anything in his heart; you go I shall come after sometimes." Replied Animesh.

That annoyed Minister's man and he threw a lot of abuses on him and went away threatening with dire consequences. He finished his work which took about half an hour and thereafter came to see the Minister but there was an altogether different scene existing. Two cardiologists from some other hospital had been called and they were examining him. Animesh silently watched the proceedings at the end of which they advised him for coronary angiography and to be shifted to CCU (cardiac care unit). He could understand that all the exercise was nothing but a drama to satisfy the ego of the VIP (very important person) but in turn he would be wasting a valuable space in CCU, which could otherwise be availed by some genuine patient. Next day again the drama was repeated, Minister was taken to catheterisation theatre and coronary angiography conducted on him and he was made to watch real time procedures on the TV monitor and was explained that there was nothing wrong on the cardio-vascular front. He remained in that hospital for a week's time and every day some drama was enacted along with the treatment for the actual problem. When VIP felt that he had been cured only then did he leave the hospital. The drama and all related business irked Animesh but he had to remain a mute spectator and he felt whole episode nothing but an insult to medical profession.

It was a Saturday afternoon that Animesh got a ring from Anjali informing him that Ratnesh had come to see them. He left all that he was engaged in and proceeded to his house where his friend had already been taken care of by his wife. Both the friends hugged each other and expressed their delight to be together once again. Ratnesh was having some luggage which was placed in the guest room and they preferred to take some coffee together during which Anjali joined them.

"I have finally made up my mind to renounce the worldly life and go to my father's monastery and hopefully this is my last meeting with you both. In fact, I feel satisfied that I could be with you for some times and my mother could meet you both and left the world satisfied." Said Ratnesh.

"But this is the most painful episode for me, whether you were near to me or not I had satisfaction that an old friend of mine is with me."

"That is true but at length destiny has struck me and I have to obey her command."

"Ok, but what is your plan?"

"To-night I will be with you and to-morrow morning I like to go away."

"That is not acceptable to me. You say this is our last meeting then let us be together for as much time as possible."

"Ok, to-morrow evening, because the last train goes in the night at ten hours and I would like to catch that. In fact, I don't know the exact location but I hope I will find that out."

Animesh asked him to freshen up and he also went for a change. He asked Anjali to prepare food of his choice, all Gujarati cuisine whatever Ratnesh liked. After half an hour all the three went out for a small stroll remembering the days how both the friends used to roam on the roads whenever they were free.

Anjali had cooked a variety of items about which Ratnesh had expressed liking whenever they had met earlier. During dinner Ratnesh liked to listen more about Anjali and her likes and dislikes, particularly what she liked in the present set up of things. She had never seen this country from a grown up eyes and obviously knew nothing but she was not having any feeling or repulsion as she found people to be good. The things which she disliked was the absence of a system, absence of public cleanliness, self-centred approach and of course diversity of social & economic levels. Though she had a fancy for US but somehow she felt an attachment with the soil and had there been some close relatives in this country she would have preferred to continue here. She described how had she felt when she went to visit the place where her parents had lived and she had spent four years of her childhood. When she saw the relics of the house of her parents she had cried and felt that every piece of that house was pulling her to itself with an invisible thread of emotional link. She had paid obeisance to that place and after staying there for a couple of hours had left back with a very heavy heart. Oh God! She could not understand where from such a strong pull she had felt at that place on that day. Anjali also narrated many things about her ladies' club and the affectionate behaviour of Mrs. Niranjan who used to give her a motherly touch.

Next day from morning onwards both the friends were extremely busy in different activities and they had the lunch together remembering many things of their childhood past; which was a dream in imagination and no video clipping was possible to share. Anjali was quite busy in household work and preparing breakfast and lunch etc but occasionally she would share what all good & painful they had in their memory storage but one thing she could make out very clearly that both the friends were products of their circumstances which ran parallel for many years and then got diversified. She had heard them several times talking of fate and destiny. Though she did not intervene but she could not appreciate that in the modern day life when people could do what they liked with meticulous planning and directed efforts.

The evening was approaching and she could notice Ratnesh and Animesh both getting restive as if a bomb shell was to explode. The happiness which was on their faces and the way they had been chit-chatting so far was fading away. Was it a sign of something lurking or just a fear of their going on separate path with no hope to meet again? Anjali had developed a brotherly feeling for Ratnesh and she also felt that something started hammering her mind with so many bizarre thoughts. As it was dusk time Ratnesh liked to proceed but Animesh asked him to take dinner and thereafter he would take him in his car to railway station and see him off. Anjali also insisted for the same and went to the kitchen to prepare a simple dinner and also to make a packet of eatables and water bottle for use during his long journey. Animesh without telling anything to Ratnesh had already asked one of his well-known person to make a reservation in AC (air conditioned) two tier sleeper coach under emergency quota to ensure that Ratnesh had a comfortable journey from his place onwards and had made his mind to tell that and give him ticket only on reaching the railway station.

At eight hours in the night they came to dining table to have their last supper before bidding him adieu from the worldly life to become a Sanyasi thereafter. As they finished the meals all the three became emotional and their voice got choked. They all found themselves at a loss to speak something to each other. Anjali had lost her mother and father, had relinquished everything given to her by her father but she had never felt so emotional as she was feeling then. It was an extremely painful moment to allow him to take his baggage and accompany Animesh to go to his car for onward sojourn. Animesh asked Anjali if she liked to accompany him to railway station but she had lost her courage to depart someone so near & dear. Animesh took the car out of the garage, opened the back door and placed his baggage on the back seat. He then opened the front doors of the car and asked Ratnesh to enter through left door and occupy the front seat by his side. The final moment had come and Ratnesh was to leave, Anjali started weeping and sobbing and with a lot of difficulty she could speak only,

"Will we really never meet again?"

<u>xxxxxxx</u>

EPILOGUE

Anjali and Animesh, both were totally broken down. The pangs of pain which they had received with the departure of Ratnesh away from worldly life leaving them in a lurch was unbearable and their life was changed. Anjali was performing her jobs as if she was in sleep and moving involuntarily. Animesh though busy with surgical operations assigned to him on day-to-day basis but his associates noticed him committing small-small errors whereas he was known and identified for his skill and meticulous hand precision. They could feel that something was disturbing him but who could find that out, was beyond any body's guess. A few months passed by without any sign of reverting back to earlier life. Anjali was sometimes going to ladies' club but the ebullience with which she was interacting with other ladies was missing. Mrs. Niranjan had also noticed that change but she thought that might had been because of her son whom she had been missing all those days. One evening while sipping tea in the balcony Anjali asked Animesh.

"From our house to railway station it takes a driving time of about forty-five minutes. Could you talk something why did Ratnesh suddenly decide to relinquish the organisation he was associated with and the worldly life."

"Yes. I was also very curious to know that and I specifically asked him and he only said that he had lost all charm in life and had seen his father one day in the dream who told him that his journey in the worldly life was over and he had to follow the path as planned by God for him and that prompted him to move on the path of his father."

"Did he know where was he to go?"

"Yes. His father guided him in the dream. He has got an idea and as he moves ahead some divine force will be guiding him. He is very confident to reach the monastery he has to go."

"So, he will become a Sanyasi once he reaches his monastery?"

"That is what he has decided."

"Will he be able to see us and sometimes be with us?"

"He told me that he will always be with us in an invisible form and guide our actions."

"Ok. Let me hope whatever decisions we take hereafter will be the best."

Life never stops, it moves ahead in all troubles & turmoils; pleasures & pains; tremors & terrors and adjusts itself in all adversities and that has been the most discerning quality of the human race. The couple had also adjusted themselves, however, having vanished the element of life which they had earlier and the ebullience that they had while coming to their motherland.

It was the fourth week of the month of February; the weather was very pleasant with sunny days and mildly cold winds blowing across. The duration of sunshine was on increase having left behind the smaller days, chilly and shivering weather of winters. They had decided to go out somewhere on the coming Sunday to have some refreshing air and to throw away the gloom which was lingering with them for some days. Around nine hours in the morning while they were getting ready to move out there was a ring at the door- a totally unexpected ring of the bell. Reluctantly Anjali came to open the door silently rebuking the unwelcome guest. But as soon as she opened the door she was flabbergasted to see a young girl, well groomed & well dressed with an old couple behind her also properly dressed.

"Who is there at the door?" asked Animesh from within the house.

"Though face seems familiar but I am not able to recollect."

Ok. Let me come there."

Finding her unable to recognise, the girl spoke,

"Ma'm I am Nilima, whose life you had saved."

"Oh! My God! What a fool I am. I am really sorry, I could not recognise you. Please come in. Hope your grand-parents are with you. Come into our living room."

All the guests took off their foot-wears outside the door, came inside the living room and got comfortably seated in the sofa. In the meantime, Animesh also came in there. He was extremely delighted to see a new Nilima who was completely different from that whom they had attended to on one fateful night and who used to work in his clinic as a receptionist-cum-aid. A timid and shy Nilima appeared brimming with confidence and energy. Her poor grand-parents looked very different being in proper attire and groomed properly.

"Good morning Sir. Please excuse me, I have come without informing you. Looks I

have disturbed your program. We will take only sometime."

"No, no. No disturbance at all. We were feeling quite lonely for some days so we wanted a change. It is good that you have come. We will get that here itself."

"Sir shall we go back and meet you some other day."

"No, no be here. We will have lunch together and you can go back in the evening."

Anjali also supported this proposal and asked Nilima to come inside and help her. They would discuss many things while working together. Some snacks were prepared which they all took together. The old couple in their broken language expressed their gratitude for giving to their grand-daughter and to them a new life otherwise they would have been rotting somewhere in the mud, half-clad and hungry without seeing the light of the day. In fact they had treated Animesh & Anjali like divine souls, like God and their emancipator who came to them like an angel from beyond the blue skies. They discussed and shared many horrors of poverty and village life and how forlorn a person becomes when he does not have two ends meet. Many hidden facets of life came to them with which they were not familiar and no media had ever covered them.

A simple lunch had been prepared more or less on lines with that of village life. The old couple was neither familiar with dining table & chairs nor had liking for that and therefore all preferred to sit on ground over folded carpet and take food in big plates akin to Thali serving. After the lunch was over they had their wash and they all assembled on the front terrace. Old couple remained silent and it was only Nilima who satisfied the queries of Animesh & Anjali.

"I completed my training in the Nurses Training Institute where you had got me admitted. I underwent thereafter an internship for six months during which period I was getting some money as stipend which was enough for my expenses and something I used to remit to my grand-parents also. That slowly brought change in

their life. I applied in the hospital where you were working earlier and I got a regular job based on experience in your clinic as people there are having great respect for you. I got a self-contained room in the nurses' hostel and brought my grand-parents. Slowly they are learning how to live in a city, however, they get baffled if I take them out whenever I am free.

Sir, whatever life I have got is due to you and you will continue to be an idol of worship for me and my grand-parents. These people like to go to village for some days and we decided to meet you before they go back."

They remained there till four hours in the evening and thereafter left. Though a small event but it rejuvenated Animesh & Anjali and they felt like having come back to vitality. The couple liked to relax and go to their favourite restaurant for dinner. That night they had talk with their son Arvind on Skype and expressing their happiness with his progress, asked him to get married and be settled. They desired to speak to the girl and her parents and other family members on Skype. Arvind was astonished to see a change in the behaviour of his parents and could not understand how such a transformation had taken place in them.

Animesh was completing surgery of all cases which he had approved till then but was not ready to take any new case that was irking the hospital superintendent, however it was not clear why was he doing so. Some cases were very complicated and his associates were quite apprehensive the way he had been behaving those days but he did meticulously precise surgery of all those cases with cent per cent success. An influential person, close to superintendent, had brought a case which he wanted him to operate upon but he declined saying that his services were meant for really needy people and that case was not so serious. That caused a tiff between Animesh and the hospital superintendent. Under some other pretext superintendent called him on one day in his cabin and rebuked him. Animesh came back to his cabin and immediately tendered his resignation and sent a fax to prime minister's office to that effect. Superintendent realised his mistake and liked him to take back his resignation but Animesh stuck to his point and went away from the hospital without worrying whether his balance amount of emoluments were paid to him or not.

He asked Anjali to pack up and be ready to go back within a week's time. Niranjan couple were grieved to know of their departure. However, Animesh & Anjali pacified them by citing their son's request and extending them an open invitation to be their guest whenever they visited States.

Nilima was keen to be with them upto the airport to see them off as she may not get another opportunity to meet them but they wishing all the best, advised her to take care of a baby girl whenever she could and that would be the biggest remembrance of them.

While couple was flying in the plane towards States many thoughts and experiences were stirring their mind but they had the satisfaction that,

"Their coming to motherland was not a waste."

ABOUT THE BOOK

"Coming to motherland was not a waste", was the only point of their satisfaction.

An India born American doctor comes to India along with his India born American professional wife to serve his motherland and the needy people, responding to the clarion call given by the top leadership of the country.

He finds India though developing yet saddled with evils of the past which have taken newer shapes while poor retaining the value systems but affluent and political personalities controlling the show in their own way.

He finds one of his closest friends who has been a victim of circumstances and the materialistic attitude of the people around him and who ultimately decides to leave the worldly life to become a sanyasi.

Animesh and his wife Anjali are also not happy with the things going on around them and the departure of their friend gives them a terrible jolt. However they had been able to bring up a poor girl and her elders and that gives them a solace when they are returning back to States.

ABOUT THE AUTHOR

Author is well known for writing on contemporary Indian society and its problems including corrupt practices in the defence.

He is a doctorate in chemistry and has served Government of India in various capacities for thirty-five years particularly in the field of defence high energy materials and warfare stores, however, after leaving his government job he is devoting his time for the cause of defending & protecting human rights as a self-less service.

He has published about a dozen books through Create Space self-publishing written in Hindi and English. Some of his famous books are Kaikeyi(Hindi), An Odyssey of Odds, Beyond the Barren Lands, The Fragrant Soil and A Carpet of Wounds.

www.ingramcontent.com/pod-product-compliance
Lightning Source LLC
Chambersburg PA
CBHW060516290526
45791CB00001B/414